Espresso for a Woman's Spirit

Book 2

Espresso for a Woman's Spirit

Book 2

More Encouraging Stories of Hope and Humor

PAM VREDEVELT

Multnomah® Publishers *Sisters, Oregon*

ESPRESSO FOR A WOMAN'S SPIRIT BOOK 2
published by Multnomah Publishers, Inc.
© 2001 by Pam Vredevelt

International Standard Book Number 1-57673-986-4

Cover design by The Office of Bill Chiaravalle
Cover art by Michael Crampton/Mendola Ltd.

Unless otherwise noted, Scripture quotations are taken from *The Holy Bible,* New International Version © 1973, 1984 by International Bible Society. Used by permission of Zondervan Publishing House.
Also quoted: *The Message* © 1993 and *The Message: Old Testament Books*
© 1996 by Eugene H. Peterson
The Living Bible (TLB) © 1971 used by permission of Tyndale house Publishers, Inc. All rights reserved
The Holy Bible, King James Version (KJV)
New American Standard Bible (NASB)®, © 1960, 1977, 1995 by the Lockman Foundation
Holy Bible, New Living Translation (NLT), © 1996. Used by permission of Tyndale House Publishers, Inc.
All rights reserved.
The Amplified Bible (AMP) ©1965, 1987 by Zondervan Publishing House
The Holy Bible, New King James Version (NKJV) © 1984 by Thomas Nelson, Inc.

Printed in the United States

For information:
Multnomah Publishers, Inc. • P.O. Box 1720 • Sisters, Oregon 97759

Library of Congress Cataloging-in-Publication Data
Vredevelt, Pam W., 1955–
    Espresso for a woman's spirit: encouraging stories of hope and humor / by Pam Vredevelt.
        p. cm.
    Includes bibliographical references.
    ISBN 1-57673-986-4
    1. Christian women—Religious aspects—Anecdotes. 2. Christian women—Religious life—Humor. 3. Christian women—Conduct of life—Humor. 4. Women—Spiritual healing. I. Title
    BV4527.V74 2000
    248.8'43—dc21
    00-008959

01 02 03 04 05 06 07—10 9 8 7 6 5 4 3 2 1 0

To John,
my best friend and partner in life.

Contents

Contents

Acknowledgments

I want to recognize an invaluable team of people who helped make this book a reality:

Thank you, my dear friends and acquaintances, for entrusting me with the privilege of sharing your stories. Your personal accounts point to the never-ending love and good humor of God.

Thank you, Don and Brenda Jacobson, for all you've done to encourage and release my writing. I am deeply grateful for the privilege of working with your top-of-the-line team.

Thank you, Multnomah family, for your enthusiasm and investment in the Espresso for Your Spirit series. Without your dedicated efforts, the wonderful stories in these books would still be sitting in a file on my desk.

Thank you, Holly Halverson, whom I have recently nicknamed "My Whiz Kid Friend." Your superb organization and crisp editing skills have enhanced the flavor of each story. I appreciate your devotion to serving the reader only the best of the best.

And finally, thank you my family and friends, for your hugs, prayers, and support while I have labored on this manuscript. Next to the Lord, you are the greatest joy of my life.

INTRODUCTION

A Sip to Get You Started

One of the fun things about being an author is the letters I receive from people who have read my books. It always encourages me to know that a story I've told has somehow made a difference in another person's life. Every now and then I set aside an evening after the children are in bed, fix myself a warm mug of decaf, and nestle into a chair by the fire to read letters from readers.

Recently I received some feedback that made me chuckle. One lady from the Midwest wrote, "Pam, I read your book *Empty Arms: Emotional Support for Those Who Have Suffered Miscarriage, Stillbirth, and Tubal Pregnancy* fifteen years ago. I just finished your book *Espresso for Your Spirit: Hope and Humor for Pooped Out Parents*. My how time has changed things. You've gone from having empty arms to being a pooped out parent!"

Yep, she was right.

I suppose many books are birthed from a personal need. That is the case for the book you are holding in your hands. After the second book in the Espresso series was released, *Espresso for a Woman's Spirit: Encouraging Stories of Hope and Humor,* I began receiving letters from women across the country who said that they were reading the book to their husbands and children and wanted to know if a sequel would follow. One radio talk-show host said that he and his wife had a nighttime routine of reading in bed before turning out the lights and that the two of them fought over who was going to get to read *Espresso* first. Even though I suspect that he was making an extra effort to make me feel welcome on his show, it did my heart good to know that people were vying to get their hands on something I had written. (I know it's a far cry from the Harry Potter phenomenon that has swept the nation, but hey—it still puts a smile on my face!)

In September, the media campaign for *Espresso for a Woman's Spirit* began, and more requests evolved. One talk-show host after another asked me, "So, Pam, when are you going to write another Espresso book?"

That started me thinking...and then dreaming...and then writing—and *Espresso for a Woman's Spirit, Book 2* began to take shape. In this book I have taken great pains to select stories that will warm your heart and encourage your spirit. Whether you are single or married, an employee or an employer, a student, a parent, or not, I think you'll find yourself energized by these true stories. Like those in the first two books in the Espresso series, they are excerpts from the lives of ordinary people, like you and me, who have encountered God in a dramatic, life-giving way. Although some names have been changed for the sake of privacy, the stories depict the events as they really happened.

We live in a world filled with bad news. It is my goal to deliver some good news: God loves you and cares about those things—large and small—that really matter to you. I also want to remind you, my friend, that God is mightily at work both in this world and in you: in your place of employment, in your family, in your studies, in your friendships, in your circumstances.

In this smorgasbord of stories, you will meet people who, in the midst of their daily grind (pun intended!), have discovered themselves on holy ground. God has intercepted them in powerful and compelling ways—through the Scriptures, through circumstances, through dreams, and through other people. And the result? They were never the same again.

Someone once said, "The hardest thing about life is that it is so daily." It never lets up. In the day in which we live, all kinds of stresses drain our energy reserves. Life has a way of shooting holes in the bottom of our cup and leaving us empty.

Is your spirit thirsty? Does your soul crave something that the things of this world won't satisfy? If so, come with me. Let's go to the Fountain of Life, fill our cup to over-flowing, and sip to our heart's content. Jesus said, "Whoever drinks of the water that I will give him shall never thirst; but the water that I will give him will become in him a well of water springing up to eternal life" (John 4:14, NASB).

On the following pages you will find warm mugs of encouragement brimming with God's love, joy, mercy, and grace. Let's drink deeply.

With love (and a latte) for the journey,

Pam Vredevelt

Chapter 1

Starstruck

*J*esus said, "And surely I am with you always, to the very end of the age."

Matthew 28:20

I plopped down in the seat facing Jimmy and placed my hands on the table between us, hoping his magic would transform my chipped nails into fashionable works of art. Jimmy is a superb manicurist, and on this particular day he had his work cut out for him. We had just returned from rafting and camping in the Oregon wilds, and my poor hands looked—well—weathered.

I've been seeing Jimmy for about four years. *Oops*—let me rephrase that lest I leave the wrong impression. Jimmy has been doing my nails a couple of times a month for the last four years. We usually make small talk during the half hour it takes him to paint my nails, but on this particular day he said something that caught me by surprise. Looking up from his work, he said good-bye to a woman walking out the door. Then he turned to me and said, "That lady just lost a baby."

In the four years I'd known him, he had never commented to me about someone else in the salon.

"She came in to have her nails done a while back, obviously pregnant," he explained. "Then the next time she was wearing normal clothes." Come to find out the woman was four months along when she lost her footing on the stairs while she was carrying a basket of laundry. The baby didn't survive the fall.

Jimmy didn't know that the first book I ever wrote was for those who had suffered miscarriage or stillbirth. *This is a divine setup,* I thought. *If I had come to the salon fifteen minutes earlier or later, or if that woman had come earlier or later, we wouldn't be having this conversation.*

"I have a book I'd like to share with her," I said. "If I bring it to you, would you be willing to pass it on?"

Jimmy nodded. And he did.

I don't believe for a minute that this occurrence was a random coincidence or simply a casual conversation. I believe that God orchestrated the series of events. He knew that there was a grieving woman who needed some words of comfort and hope, and He set things up to bless her. Purpose and design were manifest in the mundane events of her day and mine. I heard later from Jimmy that the woman was very grateful and started reading the first chapter while getting her nails done. The serendipitous event reminded me of a statement I've heard my mentor make on more than one occasion: "Either everything has meaning, or nothing has meaning."

The point came home to me again the following day when I talked with a friend about her latest camping trip. While she was out in the middle of the woods, God had snagged Gretchen's attention in a rather dramatic fashion. I'll let her tell the story.

My family didn't go camping when I was young. My mother was a travel agent, so our family vacationed in hotels. She taught me how to pack a bag for overseas travel by rolling the items rather than folding them, but I never learned how to make trail mix or to pack the essentials for life in the woods. So I had a lot to learn when my husband, Kevin, announced that he wanted our family to go camping during the children's summer break.

I've learned a few things during the trips we've taken. Although I'm still a novice compared to many, I now know the importance of packing books, crayons, and games, just in case it rains for three days straight. I've learned that two rolls of paper towels are better than one (I won't go into the details concerning my toddler's bout with the flu one trip). And I've learned that a cup of steaming coffee first thing in the morning tastes better at dawn in the woods than it does in the kitchen at home. But the best lesson I learned while camping happened late this summer, when our family set up tent in Boardman, Oregon.

Although we were having a nice time, I was restless. Worries about pending changes at work crowded out my peace. I work part-time at a law firm, and my caseload had been unseasonably heavy. I was anxious about meeting pressing deadlines without compromising the quality of my work, and I was trying to adjust to a new administrator whose management style was very different from his predecessor's. Questions darted back and forth in my mind: *Will I be able to handle the policy changes gracefully? Will I be able to meet deadlines without robbing my family of what they need from me?*

I was also in the middle of coordinating our church's annual women's retreat. More questions bubbled to the surface: *Will enough women want to attend? Will their needs be met? Will our fund-raising event be successful?*

Anxieties about my children added to my tension. I wondered how they would do at their new school this fall. I hoped their teachers would instruct them well and that we would be able to handle the added financial load.

I tried my best to push these intrusive and troublesome ideas to the back of my mind, but it was useless. They continued to appear front and center.

One evening we were sitting around the campfire stargazing. We pointed to various constellations and passed the binoculars back and forth to get a better view of the Milky Way. I spotted a satellite and watched it flicker across the sky against the velvety black backdrop of night.

"Isn't it amazing that God can throw a star across the sky?" I said to my family. That question had barely left my lips when another popped into my mind: *If you can trust Me to toss a star, why can't you trust Me with the things that trouble you?*

I knew that the Spirit of God was speaking to me.

Oh, dear heavenly Father, I prayed, *You made each of these stars. You are awesome and powerful. I'm so sorry that I've been so worried.* I thought some more about my need to trust and how easy it is for me to doubt and to be like those who James said "worry their prayers":

If you don't know what you're doing, pray to the Father. He loves to help. You'll get his help, and won't be condescended to when you ask for it. Ask boldly, believingly, without a second thought. People who "worry their prayers" are like wind-whipped waves. (James 1:5–6, *The Message*)

Wiping my eyes, I changed my approach. *Lord, I need a boost to my faith,* I confessed. *Could You please show me a shooting star tonight?* I asked with a longing that ached to be filled.

I don't remember ever having asked God for something

that immediate and tangible. My boldness surprised me, leaving me feeling a tad guilty for being presumptuous. *Lord, I don't mean to test You. I just need You to be real to me.*

On the heels of that prayer, the most magnificent star began a dazzling descent across the sky. It was unlike any shooting star we had ever seen. The tail was like that of a comet, and the star moved so slowly across the sky that it looked as if it were suspended in air. We all stood like statues, captivated as the radiant ball of fire burst into two pieces before vanishing off the horizon.

I stood speechless, stunned, my eyes fixed on the sky. It was difficult to grasp what I had just witnessed. Then, as if that weren't enough, three more stars shot across the midnight sky right before our eyes. Full of vacationers, the whole campground erupted in spontaneous applause.

And the Spirit of the Lord drove home His point: *Gretchen, do you know who I am? Do you know what I can do? What do you want to ask of Me? Ask Me. Trust Me.*

Things have been different for Gretchen since that night. She's has been trusting God more and worrying less. A series of flaming stars burned a lesson deep into her psyche: God is with her every moment of every day, and He wants her to trust Him with every detail of her life.

A few days after she and her family returned from their trip, Gretchen told a friend what had happened that spectacular night out in the woods. Her friend's response was, "Wow—what a coincidence!"

Webster's dictionary says that a coincidence is an accidental occurrence of events. Did you know that the word *coincidence* is not in the Bible? The term is foreign to the Spirit of God. Why? Because He is a God of purpose; He is a God of design, order, and intention. *Nothing* in our lives is insignificant or irrelevant in the eternal scheme of things. God has a plan, and He is working it out in the midst of the daily grind of life. He is tangibly present everywhere:

In the bustling activity of a nail parlor.
Deep in the woods under a midnight sky.
And with you, wherever you are at this very moment in time.

When Jesus said, "Surely I am with you always,"
He meant *always.*
Will you look for Him today?

Power Perks: A Sip of Hope and Humor

Two elderly women were cruising along in a large car. Both could barely see over the dashboard. In time they came to an intersection. The stoplight was red, but they went on through.

I must be losing it, the woman in the passenger seat thought to herself. *I could have sworn we went through a red light.*

After a few more minutes they came to another intersection. Again, the light was red; again, they went right through. Now the woman in the passenger seat was getting nervous, and she decided to pay very close attention at the next intersection to see what was going on.

Sure enough, at the next intersection the light was definitely red, and they went right through. She turned to the other woman and said, "Mildred! Did you know we just went through three red lights in a row? You could have killed us!"

Mildred turned to her and said, "Oh dear, am I driving?"

Old age ain't no place for sissies.

Bette Davis

Power Perks: A Sip of Hope and Humor

Trust GOD from the bottom of your heart; don't try to figure out everything on your own. Listen for GOD's voice in everything you do, everywhere you go; he's the one who will keep you on track.

Proverbs 3:5–6, *The Message*

Don't burn out; keep yourselves fueled and aflame. Be alert servants of the Master.

Romans 12:11, *The Message*

The One who called you is completely dependable. If he said it, he'll do it!

1 Thessalonians 5:24, *The Message*

Whatever God has promised gets stamped with the Yes of Jesus.

2 Corinthians 1:20, *The Message*

CHAPTER 2

Just to Keep Things Percolatin'

She is clothed with strength and dignity;
she can laugh at the days to come.

Proverbs 31:25

How many of us are like the Proverbs 31 woman, who could laugh at the future? Do you face it expectantly? Anxiously? Angrily? Hopefully? Many of us, I'm afraid, have been too stung by past surprises to look at the future—or even the present—without some apprehension. But there are those who seem to be able not to take things so seriously, who have mastered the art of seeing the funny side of life. My friends Bonnie Kopp and Connie Griffith are like that. Identical twins, these gals love to handle life with lots of humor. They instinctively recognize that their love of laughter is a God-given coping mechanism for making life fun and more interesting. During their teenage years, Bonnie and Connie would go on double dates and midway through the evening swap clothes in the ladies' room. When they returned to their dates pretending to be each other, even their boyfriends couldn't tell them apart!

The twins are now in their fifties, and this healthy sense of fun continues even as one of them faces one of life's most draining experiences: serious illness. After a visit from this dynamic duo, the radiology lab at Emanuel Hospital has never been the same! See if Bonnie's story doesn't give you some ideas for replenishing your cup during difficulties.

After I was diagnosed with breast cancer, I received radiation treatment five days a week for six weeks. About midway through the process, my twin sister, Connie, called to say that she was going to pass through town for a brief visit on her way to an overseas assignment in India. This would be the last chance I'd have to see her for a very long time.

The circumstances were less than ideal. I was extremely fatigued from the radiation and a bit discouraged by the daily ordeal of having to visit the cold, sterile radiation lab. The atmosphere there was morbidly solemn; a sense of death lurked in every corner. Most of the people walking in and out of the place seemed stunned, not knowing whether they were going to live or die. The hospital personnel worked with dying people every day and were fairly desen-sitized. Whenever I arrived for my appointment, the staff made minimal eye contact with me. The nurses focused strictly on the task at hand, dedicated to keeping the patients on schedule and the medical interventions correct.

The night Connie arrived I felt inspired. I'd had enough doom and gloom in that radiation lab. It was time to liven up the atmosphere and give those nurses a shot of good ol' down-to-earth fun. I concocted a plan and asked Connie if she would be my accomplice. Usually she would have jumped at the chance to pull a twin switch, but she was a bit uncomfortable doing it to professionals and people we really didn't know. Plus, being around radiation kind of scared her. But with a little cajoling on my part, she reluctantly agreed.

(Before I tell you any more, you need to know that early in my treatment, the nurses had tattooed small dots on my chest where the radiation was to be administered. These marks are permanent. Okay, read on!)

While driving to the hospital the next morning, we asked God to please deposit some of His life and joy in that place of death. When we arrived, the nurses were busy with business behind the counter and didn't notice that instead of one, two of us had entered. We went directly to the changing room, where I gave Connie my gown. Then I coached her on the procedure.

"After you change, go into the waiting area and stay put

until a nurse comes to get you. She'll take you into the radiation lab. When you get to the lab, climb up on the table, lie down, and raise your arm above your head."

Connie played along. I watched from inside the dressing room with the light off and the door slightly ajar. I wasn't about to miss seeing our scheme unfold.

A nurse arrived right on schedule and greeted Connie. "Good morning. How are you doing today?"

"Oh, it's been such a busy morning, I'm feeling a little confused," Connie replied.

"Well, just follow me," the nurse instructed.

Connie hopped up on the table, lay down, and lifted her arm over her head per my instructions. But there was a problem. The next thing Connie heard was, "My goodness. You *are* confused! Your head is at the wrong end of the table!"

Connie was so rattled by the obvious mistake that her hands began to tremble, making it hard for her to undo her gown for the next step in treatment. The nurse was quick to pick up on it and remarked, "You're not only confused; you're nervous!"

Playing along, Connie said, "I just don't know what's wrong with me. I'm obviously not myself today."

I snickered from my hiding place.

Next the nurses needed to align the beams of light with the tattoos. But the marks were nowhere to be found. The nurse shrieked, "There are no tattoos!"

One of the other nurses, who had worked in the lab for more than five years, came running. "I've never seen anything like this before!" she exclaimed.

The two of them carefully searched for the dots. They paused only to look at each other with eyes the size of golf balls.

That was about the time I very nonchalantly walked out of the dressing room and addressed the staff from behind in a stern tone of voice: "What are you doing, giving radiation to the wrong patient?"

The technician almost fainted, and one of the nurses screamed: "There are two of you!" The rest of the staff erupted into such hilarious laughter they could hardly catch a breath.

After the giggles subsided, I switched places with Connie, and—sure enough—the dots were right where they had been the day before. I continued the treatment while Connie changed her clothes and took a seat in the waiting room. A man who was waiting for his wife wanted to know what all the laughter was about in the other room. Connie related the story. He was almost falling out of his chair with laughter when his wife walked in. This piqued her curiosity and she, too, wanted an explanation. When Connie told her what we had done, she doubled over in guffaws. Then Connie noticed tears streaming down the husband's face. When he was finally able to regain composure, he hugged his wife tightly and said to Connie in a shaking voice, "Thank you. Thank you for doing this. My wife thinks that she is dying, and this is the first time I've seen her laugh in three months."

The doctor administering my treatment turned to me and said, "You brought more healing today than any radiation could ever deliver. Thank you for being brave enough to pull the switch—and for giving everyone a good, hard laugh!"

X marks the spot. Mission accomplished.

Power Perks: A Sip of Hope and Humor

The woman's husband had been slipping in and out of a coma for several months, yet she had stayed by his bedside every single day. One day when he came to, he motioned for her to come nearer. As she sat by him, he whispered, his eyes full of tears, "You know what? You have been with me through all the bad times. When I got fired, you were there to support me. When my business failed, you were there. When I got shot, you were by my side. When we lost the house, you stayed right here. When my health started failing, you were still by my side. You know what?"

"What, dear!" she asked gently, smiling.

"I think you're bad luck."

Some people completely quench their thirst at the Fountain of Life. Others simply gargle.

My boss was complaining in our staff meeting the other day that he wasn't getting any respect. Later that morning he went to a local sign shop and bought a small sign that read, "I'm the Boss." He then taped it to his office door.

Later that day when he returned from lunch, he found that someone had taped a note to the sign that said, "Your wife called, and she wants her sign back!"

Behind every successful woman…is a substantial amount of cappuccino.

Julie Woodside

The phrase "working mother" is redundant.

Jane Sellman

You revive my drooping head; my cup brims with blessing.

Psalm 23:5, *The Message*

CHAPTER 3

A Risk Worth Taking

*M*y dear children, let's not just talk about love; let's practice real love. This is the only way we'll know we're living truly,
living in God's reality. It's also the way to shut down debilitat-
ing self-criticism, even when there is something to it.

1 John 3:18–20, *The Message*

Ever since our son, Nathan, was born with Down's syndrome, we have become acquainted with a whole new
group of people. Little boys and girls with special physical
and mental challenges and their parents are now an important part of our world. They support us. They comfort us.
They challenge us. And they teach us incredible lessons
about love and life.

Craig and Jennifer Sax and their little boy have done all
of those things for us. Their son, also named Nathan,

seemed an unlikely choice to be one of God's spokespeople, but this little boy left an indelible mark on the lives he touched, including mine. I'm now convinced that the life of a child can teach us as much as the life of a sage.

I met Jennifer through my friend Bonnie Knopf. As we talked over coffee one afternoon, Bonnie spoke of her deep friendship with Jennifer and told me that I just had to meet her. The following week Jennifer and I talked over the phone, sharing with each other the joys and challenges of raising a child with special needs. I sent her the stories of our Nathan in *Angel Behind the Rocking Chair,* and she sent me some pictures of her Nathan during various stages of his life.

This little guy could be on the front of a Gerber's baby food jar, I mused while flipping through several of his baby pictures. Nathan had round, rosy cheeks, big blue eyes, and a smile that would melt the hardest of hearts. He was what most people would call "picture-perfect."

But as I continued through the stack of photos, the images of strength and vitality gradually turned into reflections of a weak, frail toddler. At eighteen months of age, Nathan was diagnosed with Menke's disease, a metabolic disorder that keeps the body from absorbing copper and results in brain atrophy, seizures, loss of motor control, and the inability to follow a normal growth pattern. Nathan's parents learned that throughout his life he would suffer from extremely weak and breakable bones and that he would never walk, speak, or grow like other children. His life expectancy was uncertain.

As Jennifer and I talked together, we shared battle stories. We knew that there was nothing easy about raising a child who had a handicap or a fatal disease. It was a grueling, backbreaking, grievous, long-term assignment. At times it was also a miraculous, faith-building, and even joyous experience. So although Jennifer spoke frankly of the unending emotional strain she and Craig endured, she also described the God-sized lessons their little boy taught them. If you could see the twinkle in their eyes and hear the passion in their voices as they spoke of Nathan, you'd sense something sacred about that little boy's presence in their home. Something unique and eternal. Something like a gift, not a burden.

One pivotal lesson came when Nathan was eight years old. It was just a typical day at the end of what seemed like a very long week. Work had been stressful. Burdensome household tasks were piling up in heaps. Craig and Jennifer were too tired to cook and decided that it was time someone else did the honors. Pizza sounded good. While Jennifer locked the house, Craig strapped Nathan (who was about the size of an eighteen-month-old baby) in his car seat to make the trek across town.

The smell of fresh pizza wafted through the windows of the car as they rolled into the parking lot. There was an empty space not too far from the entry. Craig pulled in and proceeded to take Nathan and the car seat out of the back.

(Nathan typically sat in his car seat in restaurants so that his body would have ample support at the dinner table.)

Things were moving along just fine until Craig accidentally brushed Nathan's foot lightly against the back of the front seat. Nathan's piercing wail turned every head in the parking lot in their direction.

Jennifer ran to help, and the couple's hearts sank. This was an all-too-familiar scenario: Even the lightest motion could fracture Nathan's bones. Sure enough, when their doctor examined Nathan, he found that the femur of his left leg was broken.

Nathan had a broken leg, and Craig had a broken spirit. He couldn't remember when he had ever been more discouraged. Angry questions ricocheted through his mind: *How could I have done this to my son? Why does something as simple as going out for pizza have to be so difficult? When will life stop being so hard?*

Jennifer tried her best to console Craig. She reminded him of the time she had picked up Nathan from the living room floor and set him on her lap. Even though his leg barely tapped the side of her thigh, it cracked like a brittle twig. She knew they both went to great lengths to prevent injury by handling Nathan's delicate body with the utmost care, but there were times when the disease dictated the outcome.

During the days following Nathan's fracture, Craig withdrew. He avoided Nathan, pulling away for fear of unintentionally hurting him again. There was no hand-holding. No hugging. No rocking. No contact. No nothing.

Every night Craig and Jennifer crawled into bed, pulled the covers up close, and prayed for sound sleep until morning. But one night it wasn't to be for Craig. A vivid dream, unlike any he had experienced before, invaded his slumbers. He was instantly aware that he had died and gone to heaven. There on the road in front of him stood his son. When he recognized Nathan, they embraced and began to walk and talk about the life they had shared on earth.

"Nathan, how was I as a dad?"

"Oh, Dad, you were great!" Nathan's face lit up with a smile.

"But, Nathan, I want you to think carefully. Was there anything I could have done that would have made me a better dad?"

Nathan paused and pondered his father's question. "Well, Dad, I guess there is one thing."

"Yes, Nathan, go ahead. Tell me what's on your mind."

"Dad, do you remember the time we went out for pizza, and you broke my leg?"

Shaking his head with a sigh of deep regret, Craig responded, "Yes, Nathan, I do."

"Dad, that wasn't all that bad, but..." His voice trailed off as he looked away.

"Yes, Nathan—go on," Craig urged.

"Dad, do you remember how after that happened, you stopped touching me?"

"Yes, Nathan, I do."

"I wish you hadn't done that, Dad."

At precisely that moment, Craig awoke a changed man. He sat bolt upright in bed, replaying the scenes from the dream in his mind. He felt certain that this had been no ordinary dream. It was a message demanding action.

Not wanting to awaken Jennifer, he quietly slipped out of bed and went into Nathan's room. Ever so gently he scooped his little boy out from under his bedcovers, placed him on his lap, and held him through the dark hours of the early morning. And from that moment forward, every single day of the rest of Nathan's life, that little boy felt the loving touch and warm caresses of his father's embrace.

Those were six of the richest years of Craig's life. Nathan's disease took his life when he was fourteen. Today Craig would give anything to be able to hold his son again. The truth is that one day he will. When his days on earth are through, Craig will pass over to the other side, and my guess is that little Nathan will be enthusiastically awaiting his arrival. That's when the humongous bear hugs will begin. Without caution. Without reserve. With total abandon. There are no broken bones in heaven. No broken relationships. No broken hearts. It's a magnificent hope that keeps Jennifer and Craig going.

As I listened to this young couple tell me their story, I found myself thinking about my own tendency to withdraw when something painful happens in a relationship. I suppose that by nature I tend to flee instead of fight. I found myself asking soul-searching questions: *Pam, who are the Nathans in your life? Is there anyone from whom you have withdrawn? Your husband? Your children? A coworker? A friend? Are you purposely avoiding someone simply because he or she has hurt you—or because you are the source of hurt?*

I remembered that good relationships take hard work. They demand risk, and if they are to last, they will involve hurt. But withdrawal is not the answer.

Let me clarify something here. Sometimes it is important and necessary to detach ourselves from people who, without conscience or regret, damage our souls. No one should ever tolerate abuse. But normal friendships have ups and downs, and sometimes, unintentionally, feelings get hurt. Sometimes we unwisely shut down these relationships because we don't want to do the tough work needed to maintain a friendship. I've certainly felt the temptation to give up instead of give in and seek restoration. So, while sometimes friends need to part for a time so they can sort out their feelings and study the conflict more objectively, detaching permanently over puny issues doesn't do anyone any good. After all, the hallmark of our faith is our love for one another—the way we make forgiveness and love our priorities in our relationships with one another.

Believe me: A pattern of withdrawal coupled with an unforgiving spirit can level relationships like a high-powered explosive levels a ten-story building. Clinical research has documented time and again that fighting and disagreements are not the bombshells that ultimately blow marriages and friendships apart—stonewalling is. Good relationships don't grow in an absence of conflict. They grow in the presence of a reconciling spirit. And a reconciling spirit takes the initiative. It reaches out. It makes repair attempts. It invites change. It risks again and again, even when it's hard.

May I ask you a simple question? Are there Nathans in your circle? If so, how about taking the initiative—how about stepping toward them rather than backing away? How about offering a kind word rather than maintaining silence? How about extending a pat on the back rather than folding your arms in retreat? How about risking love?

You never know. Yours might be the most important touch he or she will feel today, and you just might change a life.

I'm quite certain that little Nathan would agree.

Power Perks: A Sip of Hope and Humor

An eyewitness account from New York City on a cold day in December....

A little boy about eight years old was standing barefoot on the sidewalk in front of a shoe store, peering through the window and shivering with cold. A lady approached the boy and said, "My, little fellow, why are you looking so earnestly in that window?"

"I was asking God to give me a pair of shoes," the boy replied.

The lady took him by the hand, went into the store, and asked the clerk to get half a dozen pairs of socks for the boy. She also asked for a basin of water and a towel. He quickly brought them to her.

She took the little fellow to the back part of the store and, removing her gloves, knelt down, washed his little feet, and dried them with a towel. After she put a pair of socks on the boy's feet, she bought him a pair of shoes, tied up the remaining pairs of socks, and gave them to him. She patted him on the head and said, "There, little fellow, do you feel more comfortable now?"

As she turned to go, the astonished lad caught her by the hand and, looking up in her face with tears in his eyes, asked earnestly, "Are you God's wife?"

Jesus Christ served others first; He spoke to those to whom no one spoke; He dined with the lowest members of society; He touched the untouchable. He had no throne, no crown, no bevy of servants or armored guards. A borrowed manger and a borrowed tomb framed His earthly life.

Chuck Colson

Greater love has no one than this, that he lay down his life for his friends.

John 15:13

CHAPTER 4

from foreigner to friend

*C*lothe yourselves with compassion, kindness, humility, gen-
tleness and patience.

Colossians 3:12

"Finally, an hour of peace all to myself," I whispered as I
scanned the church for a vacant seat. Our baby daughter,
Jessie, was teething, and the midnight vigils were taking
their toll. I was tired and cranky and needed a break from
motherhood. Having checked Jessie into the church nursery, I settled into my seat next to John with a thirsty spirit,
eager for God to fill my cup.

No such luck. Ten minutes into the music, the little
black box on the wall started flashing 103 in bright-red
digital numbers. That was my cue that Jessie needed her
mom. I thought about ignoring it. I considered telling the
nursery workers—after church—"I was so focused on the

service that I just didn't see the signal." But my mama had taught me well. I exited as quietly as I could and found Jessie beet red, bellowing at the top of her lungs. So much for an hour of peace. I was back in boot camp, learning lessons in patience.

It was those nasty teeth again, trying to erupt through the gum line. Pulling the numbing gel from my purse, I swabbed her gums and wondered if my headache would go away if I squeezed some of the stuff on the top of my head. A few minutes later, Jessie was settled, and I found myself talking to Nancy, another mom with a teething baby. As we chatted about postpartum joys and exhaustion, the kids pushed themselves down off of our laps and played together on the floor in front of us. They cooed, giggled, gurgled, and made funny faces at each other. I'm not sure if it was love at first sight, but they definitely had fun together. And Nancy, perhaps without even realizing it, filled my cup. Just her honest confession that she, too, had days when she wanted to turn in a letter of resignation from motherhood made me feel less alone. In my slump that Sunday, Nancy was the java jolt I needed.

Though Nancy now lives more than an hour's drive away, every once in a while we go to lunch and update each other by phone and e-mail. We joke about our friendship being somewhat on hold until we're senior citizens who can leisurely rock in our chairs and chat away the hours. Neither of us has the time we want right now. But true friendship accepts the obvious constraints without resentment and allows for a natural ebb and flow in the relationship.

There are some people in this world to whom God seems to have given an extra measure of relational sensitivity. Nancy is one. Recently she told me a moving story about her life as an Olympic athlete and NBC sports commentator. Her story speaks of unselfishness, sensitivity, and the harmonious melodies of friendship. It underlines the power of compassion in an arena where everyone's main goal is to climb to the top and be number one. And it reveals one source of Nancy's idea of mercy: She learned from a master.

In August 1979, I was somewhere over the Pacific Ocean en route to Beijing, China, to cover one of the first international sporting events hosted by that country for *NBC Sports.* I was reviewing my notes and studying the biographical information on the athletes expected to attend. Books on Chinese history and culture filled my carry-on bag. The country was beginning to recover from the cultural revolution, a failed attempt by Chairman Mao Tsetung to "equalize" social classes. Though this ancient Asian country still did not allow international tourism, the winds of change were beginning to blow open the door to a Western presence. The mission for our broadcast team was twofold: to cover the athletic competition and to explain the connection between Chinese history and culture and its reemergence into the international competitive arena.

Our production manager came walking down the aisle of the 747 and handed me the itinerary for our two-week trip. There was very little downtime on the schedule. This was a unique opportunity, and we needed every available minute to complete our assignment.

Although I was flying to Beijing on professional assignment, I was also conducting a personal search. Somewhere in that city of seven million people, I hoped to find the man, who, through a crazy turn of events, had once taught me the power of bold compassion. The picture I had of him in my suitcase was several years old, his image obscured by paper worn thin, but I hoped it would help me recognize Jhou Jiasheng if I found him.

Seven years earlier, after competing in the 1972 Olympic Games, I had been chosen for the United States gymnastics team that competed against gymnasts from the Peoples Republic of China. At that time, the Chinese were in the midst of their cultural revolution. The country was closed to outside visitors, and their athletes were forbidden to participate in international events. No Chinese athletes had competed internationally since the early sixties. When President Nixon and Chairman Mao agreed to allow their national gymnastics teams to compete, the event was more than an international competition. It was a major political breakthrough and a milestone in the relationship between the two countries.

In May 1973 the Chinese sent male and female gymnastics teams to compete against the U.S. national team in New York City's Madison Square Garden. I considered it an honor to participate in such a historic event. The diplomatic receptions were a fascinating crash course in Chinese-American politics, and we were "wined and dined" with the finest the Big Apple had to offer. All the festivities and fanfare, however, could not deter me from my goal. As the highest-ranked athlete on the team, I was determined to lead our group to victory.

To gain a competitive advantage in meets, I had been taught to distance myself from my opponents. I was never to permit emotion to interfere with my concentration. Winning was my goal. Being an ambassador for improved relations between our two countries was a distant second. And while the official Chinese team motto was "Friendship First; Competition Second," you can be sure that their coaches were keeping track of every tenth of a point on every event in hope of a Chinese victory.

After the first event, the U.S. led China by about one point. I was in the running for the all-around title. When it came to the final event, floor exercise, both teams were eager to finish strong. I had not performed the way I wanted to on the balance beam and uneven bars, so I was eager to redeem myself on floor exercise.

Out on the mat, I held my opening pose, waiting for the technician to start my taped accompaniment. Much to

everyone's surprise, all that came from the speakers was sta-
tic and noise—no music. I walked off the mat, assuming
that the sound man had put the wrong tape in the machine.
Since we were alternating performances with the men, the
announcer called for the next male competitor to proceed.

After a few minutes, I was cued to try again. I went
back out on the mat only to hear the same muffled sounds
as before. I was already disappointed about my perfor-
mance on the bars and beam. Now this! There I stood,
alone in the middle of Madison Square Garden, facing the
prospect of performing my floor exercise routine with no
music, with thousands of eyes staring at me. That's like
watching TV with the volume turned off, and it would
likely cost me some important points. Realizing that this
might be my lot, I winced at the thought of letting down
my teammates. I looked questioningly at my parents in the
audience, hoping they had an extra copy of my music with
them. They didn't.

A *Sports Illustrated* account describes the next few
moments:

> There was a foul-up in the music for Nancy Thies's
> floor exercises. Twice she appeared at center mat to
> perform, only to have the taped music turn garbled
> and shrill. At last, after an emergency interpreta-
> tion, the official traveling pianist for the Red
> Chinese, a small dignified fellow named Jhou

Jiasheng, took his place at the keyboard, and as Nancy performed her complex routine, he watched carefully and composed an extemporaneous arrangement of western classical music that matched her balletic moves perfectly. It was a magnificent international duet. When it was over, Nancy…rushed to plant a pretty kiss upon the beaming cheek of Mr. Jhou, while the entire Garden audience rose to its feet in exultant applause.[1]

Those few minutes were some of the most significant moments of my gymnastics career. The competitive outcome was a mixed bag. I did not win the all-around award, but our efforts did give us the team title.

But that's not what has meant the most to me all these years. It was Mr. Jhou's demonstration of compassion. Somewhere in the midst of competitive rivalry and political differences, Jhou Jiasheng, a man from Beijing, China, decided to move beyond a national agenda and boldly stand up to help a fifteen-year-old girl from Urbana, Illinois, who desperately needed piano accompaniment.

Now, years later as a broadcast journalist, I had the unique opportunity to step into his world, as he had into mine many years before. Little did I know, as the plane landed in Beijing, what God had in store for Mr. Jhou and me.

The days in China were packed with fact-finding missions, production meetings, rehearsals, and location shoots. The evenings were filled with receptions and banquets attended by officials from the Chinese broadcasting, sports, and political arenas. I was in a world so very different from mine, one filled with fascinating Asian traditions and customs thousands of years old. As a journalist, I felt a sense of urgency to take in all that I possibly could and to collect as much information and footage as the opportunity afforded.

With little free time, I wondered if I could ever find Mr. Jhou. But one evening, after I was introduced as NBC's correspondent at a dinner banquet, several Chinese coaches who also had attended the 1973 event in Madison Square Garden approached me. They enthusiastically spoke of Mr. Jhou's accompaniment for my floor exercise routine and informed me that he was scheduled to play for some of the gymnasts at the upcoming competition. A messenger was sent to find Mr. Jhou and bring him to us.

I'll never forget the moment when Mr. Jhou walked into the arena with his wife and young son and extended the hand of friendship once again. With interpreters to assist us, we shared updates on our families, our jobs, and the many people who had made that 1973 Chinese-American competition so memorable. We exchanged pictures and gifts, laughed, and marveled at how small the world seemed at that moment. For a brief interlude, schedules and deadlines took a backseat to the renewal of relationship.

I made two more trips to China while I was working for NBC, and Mr. Jhou came to the U.S. for an international competition in Texas. On each occasion we were able to reconnect and nurture our friendship. Mr. Jhou and his wife spoke honestly about the challenges in their lives during the cultural revolution and told me that they yearned to live in the United States. Then, shortly after the massacre in Tienamen Square in Beijing, Mr. Jhou was invited to the United States on business. Given the political unrest, traveling out of the country was next to impossible for the average citizen. I was able to assist him in that effort, and eventually the doors for travel to the U.S. opened for him.

Jhou's desire to live in the U.S. was fulfilled in the summer of 1989. He, his wife, and their son settled in San Diego, where he now teaches piano. A few years ago, they accepted a long-standing invitation to visit us in our home. One of the highlights of this visit came when they and our friends gathered around the TV in our family room and watched the video replay of *ABC's Wide World of Sports* coverage of the competition in Madison Square Garden. Many of the friends present that night had prayed for the Jhou family members as they made their transition from China to America.

Later that weekend my husband and I stood in our living room and watched Mr. Jhou play a duet on the piano with our daughter. I reflected on the circuitous path this friendship had taken and the lessons it had taught me.

From Mr. Jhou I learned that a simple act of compassion has the power to turn dismal circumstances into treasured memories and lifelong friendships. As the music from the piano duet filled our living room, I realized that my floor routine in Madison Square Garden could have ended on a very sour note—or no note at all! But it didn't. Music flowed from compassion, and nearly thirty years later the duet continues, with creative new stanzas yet to be composed.

When I think about Nancy's story, it occurs to me that there is rarely a perfect or even a convenient time to offer our love and help to others. Clearly there are times when a compassionate move to assist someone may not appear to be in our best interest. Had Mr. Jhou stayed in his seat and not offered to accompany Nancy, the Chinese might have won the competition.

In highly competitive situations, where some folks establish relationships simply to ensure their own success or personal advancement, acts of compassion can be viewed with suspicion. We run the risk that cynics will interpret our caring gestures as manipulative tactics to get ahead. Some may doubt our sincerity and assume that we have hidden motives.

Then, too, our efforts to reach out may be unreciprocated or even rejected. Our kindness may be ridiculed.

Nancy's story, however, underscores the value of taking the risk to break through barriers—personal, cultural, academic, competitive—and love others anyway. It's the way of the cross:

> Remember that at that time you were separate from Christ...without hope and without God in the world. But now in Christ Jesus you who were once far away have been brought near through the blood of Christ. For he himself is our peace, who has made the two one and has destroyed the barrier, the dividing wall of hostility. (Ephesians 2:12–14)

It is also what wins God's Gold Medal of Honor.

Think today of someone who might need the java jolt only you can give, and give it. You may lift a spirit, warm a heart—or even initiate a series of similar kindnesses. A cup of compassion is always a brew worth sharing.

Power Perks: A Sip of Hope and Humor

We cannot hold a torch to light another's path without brightening our own.

Ben Sweetland

Friendship doubles our joy and divides our grief.

I love the LORD, for he heard my voice; he heard my cry for mercy. Because he turned his ear to me, I will call on him as long as I live. The LORD is gracious and righteous; our God is full of compassion.

Psalm 116:1–2, 5

"For if you give, you will get! Your gift will return to you in full and overflowing measure, pressed down, shaken together to make room for more, and running over. Whatever measure you use to give— large or small—will be used to measure what is given back to you."

Luke 6:38, TLB

When you have no helpers, see all your helpers in God. When you have many helpers, see God in all your helpers. When you have nothing but God, see all in God; when you have everything, see God in everything. Under all conditions, stay thy heart only on the Lord.

Charles Spurgeon

God comes in where my helplessness begins.

Oswald Chambers

We are all strings in the concert of God's joy; the spirit from his mouth strikes the note and tune of our strings.

Jakob Bohme

CHAPTER 5

TP from Heaven

My God will liberally supply (fill to the full) your every *need according to His riches in glory in Christ Jesus.*

Philippians 4:19, AMP

How are you today? Are you content with your life, satisfied with your work, fulfilled in your relationships? If so, I am glad for you! But this chapter will mean more to those who feel stretched beyond the breaking point, fresh out of faith, and ready to retreat.

Patty Burke, an obviously fun lady who had read one of my books, wrote to me about such a time in her own life and how God unexpectedly met her there. Her letter tickled my funny bone and put a smile on my face that reappears every time I walk down the toilet-paper aisle at the grocery store.

Let Patty's story remind you that God can—and will—do anything on your behalf! She wrote:

Dear Mrs. Vredevelt,

My life has been full of experiences where God has worked in mysterious and miraculous ways. But one humorous incident comes to mind that I thought might brighten your day.

Several years ago I was suffering with severe health problems that the doctors could not diagnose. I am a nurse, used to having high energy. But during this time of my life, I was weak, lethargic, drained of all strength, and felt like I had a perpetual flu.

My husband is a minister. During the time of my ailment, he decided it was time to resign from the church he was leading. I was used to moving from one church to another, but I worried about where we would go next.

Things went from bad to worse during the interim period between pastorates because my husband was unable to find temporary work anywhere. I was working two nursing jobs, unable to take sick leave because we had no other income. The stress of the illness and the worry over a pending move about did me in. But I had no choice other than to keep trucking along.

One Friday, between pay periods, I had only two dollars left to buy groceries. I took inventory to see what we needed most. I was out of orange juice and had only one half-roll of toilet paper left.

I reasoned that the orange juice was important for our health, so I went to the store, bought the juice, and asked God to s-t-r-e-t-c-h the TP.

The next day when I went out to our mailbox, amongst several letters I found a little square package—you know, one of those sample things. When I opened it up, much to my astonishment, there was a full roll of toilet tissue inside! I stood by the mailbox, my mouth hanging open, utterly amused by God's sense of humor and His kindness. When He says He will meet our every need, we're talking *every* need—even the ones we'd rather not mention.

Curious, I asked several other people in town and on our route if they had received sample TP in the mail. Everyone said no except one other woman. It just so happened that her husband was a preacher too. I'm not sure what to make of it, but it happened.

By the way, how many folks do you know who have had toilet paper sent from heaven?

Don't ever forget—God cares about every little detail of your life, right down to the bare necessities.

"Let him have all your worries and cares, for he is always thinking about you and watching everything that concerns you" (1 Peter 5:7, TLB).

Power Perks: A Sip of Hope and Humor

At the end of a job interview, a human resources director asked a young engineer fresh out of MIT, "And what starting salary were you looking for?"

The engineer said, "In the neighborhood of $125,000 a year, depending on the benefits package."

The interviewer said, "Well, what would you say to a package of five weeks' vacation, fourteen paid holidays, full medical and dental coverage, a company matching retirement fund for 50 percent of your salary, and a company car leased every two years—say, a red Corvette?"

The engineer sat up straight and said, "Wow! Are you kidding?" And the interviewer replied, "Yeah, but you started it."

Prayer is not overcoming God's reluctance; it is laying hold of his highest willingness.

Archbishop Richard Chenevix Trench

If all things are possible with God, then all things are possible to him who believes in him.

Corrie ten Boom

To believe only possibilities is not faith, but mere philosophy.

Sir Thomas Browne

Jesus said, "So, you believe because you've seen with your own eyes. Even better blessings are in store for those who believe without seeing."

John 20:29, *The Message*

CHAPTER 6

When Your Get-up-and-Go Gets up and Dies

*L*et's not allow ourselves to get fatigued doing good. At the right time we will harvest a good crop if we don't give up, or quit.

Galatians 6:9, *The Message*

It wasn't any single person or event that silenced Clark and Joy's hallelujah chorus that holiday season. It was a lot of little things that caved in on them like a roof with too much snow. They learned that a couple they were close to was having serious marriage problems. They had visited three people in the hospital and felt their pain. A friend had shown up on Clark and Joy's doorstep late one night, crying her heart out. Joy had tried to console her as she sorted through the crazy quilt of the young lady's love life. A few weeks earlier they had attended the funeral of a friend who died of cancer. She was only five years older than Joy.

Clark and Joy are a couple committed to helping people within a church setting. Clark pastors a Baptist church in Michigan, and he and Joy have three children: Katheryn, Clark III, and Callie. Usually they are founts of joyful giving, and Christmas to them means an extra opportunity to bless others.

But this time, it was all too much. So many needs. So many demands. So many crises. It was getting ridiculous. They began to feel like a power outlet with too many extension cords plugged in, draining off their energy. Clark remembers well a pivotal day in that season. I'll let him tell the story.

I sat on the couch, watching our three kids decorate the tree. When they asked if I wanted to help them set up the manger scene, I just sighed, forced a smile, and said, "I'm enjoying watching you guys do it this year. Go ahead." Even the Chicago Brass playing "Joy to the World" on the stereo couldn't keep me from sinking deeper and deeper into a funk.

We heard a thump against the door. Katheryn recognized the sound of the carrier dropping the mailbox lid and announced, "Mail's here." She and Callie ran to retrieve it while Clarkie adjusted the livestock in the manger scene.

"Wow, look at this one." Katheryn held up a particularly colorful, hand-decorated envelope. We had received lots of store-bought Christmas greetings that week, but this card had obviously taken some real, honest-to-goodness artistic effort. The pen and ink designs were magnificent. And the calligraphy! It was superb.

I flipped it over to see if the clever sender had included a return address. The back was adorned as beautifully as the front, including a couple of vivid stickers to hold the flap in place. Noting the name on the back, I stopped in my tracks. I cast my eyes to the ceiling and said, "Whoo, boy."

"What?" my kids asked. "Who's it from?"

"Man," I said, "I hope to goodness he's not needing a place to crash this holiday season."

"Who? Who?" the kids chimed in. I still hadn't answered their question.

"Bertrand," I said flatly.

"What kind of a name is that?" Clarkie asked.

I removed a beautiful card that had obviously been hand drawn with colorful markers. Bertrand had always been very artistic, even when he was drunk.

"Who's Bertrand?" all three kids sang in unison.

"Um," I hesitated, still staring at the card, hoping against hope that he wasn't coming to town. "Bert Thompson's a guy we knew back at the church before this one."

It wasn't a very detailed explanation, but the kids were satisfied with the answer. They filed off into the living room to look at the card while I stood in the kitchen, afraid to open the letter for fear it meant that our high-maintenance friend would burst back into our lives again. I just knew how the letter would start: "Had a little trouble with the law; need a place to stay. Would it be possible…?" We simply didn't have room for his battery cables. Everyone else had drained us dry.

I prayed quietly, *Oh, dear God, forgive me for feeling this way, but I just don't know if I have enough patience and energy to deal with this guy again. Isn't there someone else available to take on this assignment?*

Bert was one of the most intelligent and engaging personalities I knew—when he was sober. A powerful communicator, he could talk philosophy, theology, music—you name it. I remember thinking, *What's not to like about this guy?* Then his wife, Karen, told us about his "bad side." Bert had a problem with alcohol, a fact I discovered only a couple of weeks after I met him.

The pastor and I had driven over to Karen and Bert's house to see why she was so distraught. Between sobs she told us, "Bertrand came home drunk again. He's had this job for only two months. I can't count how many jobs he's lost. He just won't stay sober."

This time, though, Karen had told him that she wasn't going to let him in the house. She locked him out and told him to come back when he was sober. She shook as she said, "He found a piece of two-by-four and started whacking it against the side of the house, threatening to break the sliding glass door. He was so out of control—worse than I've

seen him in a long time. He said he was going to…"
Between wracking sobs she explained what he had threatened. In response, she had called the police.

When they showed up, he was gone. That's why she had called us. "He's out there somewhere," she said, "probably sleeping in a gutter or under a bridge. He may get arrested again, and I almost hope he does. I just don't think I can take any more. I can't keep living this way."

That was only one of many such occasions. The pastor finally arranged for Bert to work on a building project at our church for a few months, on the strict condition that he not drink. The rule was that if he stepped foot on the property and we even thought he smelled like alcohol, we would tell him to go home, as difficult and unpleasant as that might be. Tough love isn't tough on just the one being disciplined. It's tough on everyone involved.

The arrangement worked well for a few weeks. As Bert and I worked together on the new building, we listened to some of our favorite music on a boom box and swapped stories. I began to think that he might have found a place where he could stay clean and be useful.

But then one Thursday, when I was the only staff member at church, Bert showed up late for work with fifty-proof breath. I sighed, shook my head, and said, "I'm sorry, Bert, my friend, but I'm afraid you'll have to leave."

"Bertrand!" he spat out, spraying me with saliva. "Don't ever call me 'Bert'!" He tried to poke his finger into my chest but lost his balance, grabbing the doorjamb to keep from falling over. "Only my real friends call me that."

"C'mon, now. I'm your friend, too, Bertrand," I said, as calmly as I could. I was trying very hard to keep from showing how nervous I was. He was a lot bigger than me, and after hearing Karen describe his angry episodes, I was sure he could take me down.

"Oh yeah?" he said, teeth together, eyes blazing. "Well, if you were my real friend, you wouldn't be kickin' me out onto the street, now, would you? You know it's cold out there!"

It wasn't worth the effort to try to reason with him. I had tried too many times before I finally realized that there's no such thing as a rational conversation with a drunk. I decided to just stand my ground and get it over with. "You'll have to leave, Bertrand," I said sadly. "That was our agreement."

He slurred, "Yeah right. The agreement. Ha! You guys and your agreements. You're all the same. Nobody understands. Nobody. That's okay. That's just fine. If you want me to leave, I'll leave. But you can't deal with me either. Nobody can. Nobody's strong enough to know how to handle ol' Bertrand."

Bertrand had the extraordinary ability to speak the truth about others and about his own pitiful condition even when he was falling-down drunk. He was absolutely right. I didn't know how to handle him. I'd tried everything I knew and then some. Nothing seemed to work.

Bert spewed a few other choice comments on his way out the door, and I went back upstairs to calm down and try to get some work done. Later that afternoon while I was locking up, I saw a small rock placed just inside the corner door in the basement. The rock had kept the door from shutting all the way. I also smelled beer.

I closed my eyes, took a deep breath, and let it out fast. Bert was back. The question was, where?

I went searching, asking myself, *Where would I go if I didn't want anyone to find me?* My eyes landed on a closet door in the fellowship hall. It was a closet that took a ninety-degree turn and got smaller as it led under one of the stairways. When I opened the door, the stench nearly drove me back. I'd found him, all right. There was Bert, passed out under the stairs. Next to him was a half-finished bottle in a brown paper bag.

At that moment I was so mad that I wanted to sober him up just so I could smack him and yell, "I have reached the end of my caring!" Instead, I called the police, because the pastor and I had agreed to do that as part of our contract with Bertrand.

As they hauled him off, I thought, *Lord, what's it going to take? We've done everything humanly possible. We can't do any more. Please do something to reach this guy. Please, Lord.*

That was the last time I saw Bertrand. That was my last mental snapshot—his legs sticking out from under the closet stairway and the stinking bottle in the paper bag next to him. I had called the police so they could come take away my friend. Not exactly a great farewell party.

That's why, when I opened that envelope, I was afraid to read the letter inside. I didn't want to find out what kind of trouble he was in now. I was afraid that he had tracked us down through mutual friends. That had been his pattern. He would use up all his other friends' patience and then circle back around to some old ones that hadn't seen him for a while. I just knew he was making the rounds again.

It had been four years since we had heard anything about him. Joy was as curious as I was and peeked over my shoulder at the letter. I read out loud:

"Dear Clark and Joy, I've been sober now for forty-four months. I'm finishing a degree in biology so I can teach high school. I'm a wounded healer, helping lead an AA group in my church."

Neither Joy nor I could believe what we were reading.

"I just wanted you to know that I haven't forgotten all the times you prayed with me and agonized over my problems."

I had to stop a moment because my voice was about to stop working. Joy put her hand on my shoulder. I took a deep breath and continued: "I know I caused you two a lot of pain because it was obvious—"

"Oh, honey," I said, ashamed of what I had thought when I first saw the envelope. "—obvious you genuinely cared about me."

"Can you believe this?" Joy asked. I tried my best to get through the rest of the letter without completely breaking down:

"Thanks for the time, effort, and care you invested in my life. Though you didn't see it when you last saw me, your efforts really did pay off. Well, actually, it was God who did the work (but of course you know that). However, you were His instruments used to play His healing tune."

A healing tune. I shut my eyes for a moment to regain my composure, wishing I could take back all the terrible things I'd just thought about him.

Joy, seeing that I was rubbing my eyes, finished the note for me.

"I just thought I'd drop you a line to let you know how very much your care means to me. With God's great love and my grateful appreciation, Bert."

We just stood there holding the note and shaking our heads. Neither of us could speak. At the end of the note was a carefully penned postscript:

"Enjoy your Christmas. It's His season."

Bert was right. It was *His* season. Despite all the bad stuff happening around us, we could now enjoy the Christmas season.[1]

I'm pretty sure that, like Clark, we've all had days when our holiday jollies have melted in the heat of life's harsh realities. I recall a Christmas when I was so overwhelmed with grief that I didn't want to decorate a tree or wrap a single gift. The plain fact of the matter is that sometimes life is more difficult than we expect and we find ourselves in places where we really don't want to be. So we grieve. We doubt. We get mad. Engulfed in despair, our thirsty souls beg for a sip of hope or some reassurance that everything is going to be okay.

The bad news is, there are times when life in this world is very, very hard. The good news is, God promises His children that everything *is* going to be okay. He has a plan for our lives and our loved one's lives. The plan is good and cannot be thwarted by our disappointment, sadness, anger, doubts, or by others who may be the driving source of our pain. God is God, and He is in control.

It's our job to do what God asks us to do and then to trust Him with the rest. Sometimes He'll ask us to step in and speak up. Other times He'll tell us to sit tight and be quiet. But regardless of the direction He gives us, He promises to work everything out according to His plan. "And we know that God causes all things to work together for good to those who love God, to those who are called according to His purpose" (Romans 8:28, NASB). That promise stands...

- even when we're worn out and plagued by a case of the "I Don't Cares";

- even when we are confused and don't know our next step;
- even when we're big on questions and short on answers;
- even when we're scared of what lies ahead;
- even when our best efforts to help don't seem effective;
- even when our spirit is parched and we have nothing left to offer;
- even for a town drunk;
- even for you and for me.

I find great reassurance in Paul's words: "God, who got you started in this spiritual adventure, shares with us the life of his Son and our Master Jesus. He will never give up on you. Never forget that" (1 Corinthians 1:9, *The Message*).

It's the message of hope wrapped up in the story of Christmas. It's the eternal truth that quenches my thirsty spirit and energizes my depleted battery. It's the push I need to rejoin the hallelujah chorus.

Power Perks: A SIP OF HOPE AND HUMOR

An elderly woman finished her shopping. When she returned to her vehicle, she found four males in it. Dropping her shopping bags, she drew her handgun and screamed that she knew how to use it and wouldn't hesitate to do so. Then she ordered them out of the car. The four men didn't wait for a second invitation; they got out and ran like mad. The woman loaded her shopping bags into the back of the car and got into the driver's seat.

There was a small problem, however. Her key wouldn't fit the ignition.

Whoops.

Her car, an identical make and model, was parked four or five spaces away. She loaded her bags into her own car, drove to the police station, and told the sergeant on duty her story. The officer nearly tore himself in two with laughter and pointed to the other end of the counter, where four pale men were reporting a carjacking by a mad elderly woman.

No charges were filed.

One reporter asked the birthday girl what she liked best about being 102 years old. She answered, "No peer pressure."

Character cannot be developed in ease and quiet. Only through experience of trial and suffering can the soul be strengthened, vision cleared, ambition inspired, and success achieved.

Helen Keller

Consider it a sheer gift, friends, when tests and challenges come at you from all sides. You know that under pressure, your faith-life is forced into the open and shows its true colors. So don't try to get out of anything prematurely. Let it do its work so you become mature and well-developed, not deficient in any way.

James 1:2–4, *The Message*

CHAPTER 7

Is It Time to Catch the Wave?

As the body without the spirit is dead, so faith without deeds is dead.

James 2:26

Have you ever had the feeling that something is about to change? Have you ever sensed something stirring that tells you that an opportunity may be winging its way toward you?

I have. It's both exciting and frightening—the possibility of change always is. But when you know that God has initiated it, the best decision you can make is to follow His lead. When God is in the driver's seat, you can expect some hair-raising adventures and surprise blessings. The road ahead will have some twists and turns that will be unexpected, but thrilling and oh so good! Dr. Steve Stephens discovered this in a very personal way. Read on, friend.

The storm-driven waves swirled and crashed against the rocks, creating fifty-foot sprays. I was glad that Tami and I were enjoying this spectacular view from our cozy, warm suite overlooking the Pacific Ocean. Stretching out on the bed, I propped my head up on three pillows to get a better look at the majestic swells in the sea below. Captivated by the mesmerizing motions of the pounding surf, my thoughts drifted heavenward.

Lord, I'm grateful for all Your blessings, I prayed. *You have given me a wonderful wife, three great kids, a successful practice as a psychologist, and speaking opportunities. What more could a guy want?*

Yet like the surf tossing before me, restlessness also stirred within my soul. It was an unsettled feeling I couldn't quite put my finger on—something I was unable to define for myself, let alone others. *What is this longing?* I wondered. I found myself mulling over the notion that God might have something more for me to do in this world. *Lord, if there is something new You would like me to do, just show me.*

It was a short prayer, quickly said and then forgotten. Tami's voice interrupted my thoughts. "Is it almost time to go?"

Tami and I were spending a few days at the beach

with a large group of couples that had gathered together to enrich their marriages. I was the keynote speaker for four sessions that weekend, and it was time for the first one.

The crowds were gracious. After the final session, a woman named Pat approached me. "Thank you, Dr. Stephens. We appreciate your teaching very much."

I smiled and shook Pat's hand, thanking her for her kind words. Then she switched gears on me.

"I think you need to be on the radio."

I thanked Pat for her vote of confidence but dismissed the thought. After a brief walk on the beach, Tami and I returned home, back to a normal week full of activities. Everything was pretty much life as usual—at least until a few days later, when Pat called. She moved quickly to her agenda. "Steve, I work at a local radio station, and I really think you should be on the radio," she said. "Would you mind if I spoke to the station manager?"

"Well…I'm not sure," I responded, slightly taken aback. "I don't have any experience on the radio, and I think that it would be out of my comfort zone."

Pat was gracious but adamantly disagreed with my excuses and pressed the point. "Let's schedule a meeting with the manager!"

I acquiesced, figuring that nothing much would come from her request. A few days later Pat called again. "The meeting is set for this Friday!" she said with high-octane enthusiasm. "Have you thought about what sort of radio show you would like to have?"

"Not really," I said in total amazement. "But let me think about it, and we can talk more on Friday."

On Friday, I found myself with Pat and the station's general manager, brainstorming ideas for what they were forecasting as *The Dr. Steve Show*. "The show would have to air five days a week," the manager said.

I gulped hard. My life was already packed with a full-time counseling practice, my wife, and three children. Squeezing in something else, five days a week, seemed impossible.

"What time of day would you want to do a show?" the manager asked.

"I'm not sure I want a show. I've never done radio before," I said honestly.

Pat jumped in, flashing her convincing smile. "But you'd be great!"

"If you were going to do a show, what time would be best?" the manager pressed.

"I wouldn't want to take time away from my wife and children, so it would need to happen during the workday— say, sometime between 11 A.M. and 1 P.M."

The manager's face dropped, and he shook his head. I knew the suggestion wasn't going to fly. "I don't see how that could work," he said. "Those times are already booked, and they rarely open up."

"That's all right," I said, flooded by a wave of relief. "If it's meant to be, something will open up. If not, that's fine."

The meeting ended. I cordially shook his hand and left the station, thinking that the idea was dead.

Later that afternoon the phone rang. "Hello, Steve. This is Pat. Can we meet again next Friday afternoon?"

"Why?" I asked.

"A few minutes after you left the station, corporate headquarters called the station manager. There have been some schedule shifts. The 11 A.M. slot is open."

Tami just about had to peel my jaw off of the floor. Yet something inside me said that I was supposed to catch this wave and enjoy the ride.

The following Friday the general manager asked, "When can you start?"

Two months later, *The Dr. Steve Show* was born, and I was in for the ride of my life.

"Dr. Steve" has been offering encouragement, comfort, and words of wisdom over the radio airwaves every weekday for more than a year now. During his live call-in show, he answers his listeners' heartfelt questions and offers practical advice and counsel. What was at first a scary step of faith has turned into one of the most enriching experiences Steve has ever had. Each week he has the joy of interviewing top-notch communicators such as John Trent, Shirley Dobson,

Kevin Lehman, and Stormie Omartian. Steve's interaction with them has filled him up, broadened his capacity to offer more to his listening audience, and given him the chance to build friendships nationwide.

Steve's expanded ministry to his listeners has been a great source of joy too. Just last week when he was standing in a checkout line at the grocery store, the lady working the cash register said, "You know what? You sound just like Dr. Steve on the radio." When she found out that she was, in fact, talking with Dr. Steve, she went on and on about how his show had been a lifeline for her. The same thing happened when he was talking to the barber while his son was getting a haircut. Again and again he hears surprise accounts of God at work.

It's clear that Steve's new venture is a win-win situation for both him and the station. *The Dr. Steve Show* and some administrative changes have given the station a stronger financial base than ever before.

I think it's fair to say that you just never know how God is going to answer a restless prayer quietly sent heavenward in the course of a normal day. But one thing is certain. He will answer. And sometimes those answers will come...

- in ways we don't expect;
- in ways that go against the grain of human reason;
- in ways that drive us out of our comfort zones and demand risk;

- in ways that can seem much too slow, or much too fast;
- in ways that have unpredictably exciting results;
- in ways that demonstrate God is God, and we are not.

Following God's lead can be an exhilarating experience. Care to live your life to the fullest? Then go for it: Jump into the sea of faith with both feet. Launch out into the deep. Ask the Holy Spirit to have His way in your life. Then, when the high waters start to build and crest, catch the wave, and paddle like crazy. And if you don't mind, move over a bit so there's room for me. I want to risk too.

"No one's ever seen or heard anything quite like this,
Never so much as imagined anything quite like it—
What God has arranged for those who love him."
(1 Corinthians 2:9, *The Message*)

Power Perks: A SIP OF HOPE AND HUMOR

"Behold, I am the LORD, the God of all flesh; is anything too difficult for Me?"

Jeremiah 32:27, NASB

"Ask, and it will be given to you; seek, and you shall find; knock, and it will be opened to you. For everyone who asks receives, and he who seeks finds, and to him who knocks it shall be opened. Or what man is there among you who, when his son asks him for a loaf, will give him a stone? Or if he asks for a fish, he will not give him a snake, will he? If you then, being evil, know how to give good gifts to your children, how much more will your Father in heaven give what is good to those who ask Him!"

Matthew 7:7–11, NASB

God's gifts put man's best dreams to shame.

Elizabeth Barrett Browning

A burglar broke into a house one night and shone his flashlight around, looking for valuables. When he picked up a CD player to place in his sack, from the dark came a strange, disembodied voice: "Jesus is watching you."

The thief nearly jumped out of his skin; he clicked his flashlight off and froze. After a bit, having heard nothing more, he shook his head, promised himself a long vacation after his next big score, clicked the flashlight back on, and began searching for more valuables. Just as he was pulling the stereo out so that he could disconnect the wires, clear as a bell he heard, "Jesus is watching you."

Totally rattled, he shone his flashlight around frantically, looking for the source of the voice. Finally, in the corner of the room, his flashlight beam came to rest on a parrot. "Did you say that?" he hissed at the parrot.

"Yes," the parrot confessed, and then squawked, "I'm just trying to warn you."

The burglar relaxed. "Warn me, huh? Who do you think you are, anyway?"

"Moses," replied the parrot.

"Moses," the burglar laughed. "What kind of people would name a parrot 'Moses'?"

The parrot quickly answered, "The same kind of people that would name a rottweiler 'Jesus.'"

CHAPTER 8

Big Plans for a Little Boy

*W*hat is faith? It is the confident assurance that something *we want is going to happen. It is the certainty that what we hope for is waiting for us, even though we cannot see it up ahead.*

Hebrews 11:1, TLB

What nagging question hinders you today? What needling issue tugs at your faith, challenges your prayers, tests your certainty in God's goodness? Let's face it: Everyone, including Christians, encounters inexplicably painful experiences. Every person I meet can quickly recount hard times that he or she has endured. Pain is an integral part of membership in the human race.

If we're honest, most of us would have to admit that in the midst of these questions, we have struggled with tough questions about God's justice and His presence—or apparent absence. Who hasn't cried out in anguish, *God, where are You?* Who hasn't felt the gloom of disillusionment creep over his or her soul when God has seemed oblivious to prayers and the heavens silent?

Though I'm not proud to admit it, there have been times through the years when I've been tempted to throw in the towel. Keeping faith seemed too difficult, and maintaining hope seemed next to impossible. But God, in His mercy, knew my frailty and, eventually, always broke through the silence to deliver what I needed to keep on keepin' on. Sometimes the answers came through a verse in Scripture. Sometimes they came through a friend's act of love. Other times they came when God led me, through a series of events, to a paradigm shift—a change in perspective. It was as if He gave me a new pair of glasses that enabled me to see things more clearly.

I've seen Him do the same thing for others too. I want to introduce you to David and Karen, who, like you and me, have found themselves confused, bewildered, and groping through the fog of bad news in search of solutions. Their answers from heaven came in a most unexpected way, creating a paradigm shift that left them with a rock-solid assurance of God's unfailing love. Let their story remind you today that heaven is never truly silent—God is just waiting for the perfect moment to reveal His good solution to the bad problem you face.

Do we want to know beforehand if it will be a boy or a girl? This was just one of the questions Karen and I struggled with as we drove to her ob-gyn for her twenty-week ultrasound.

As Dr. Trivedi scanned the mobile form in my wife's womb, she completed her normal check-off list: ten fingers and toes, heart functioning properly. Then she asked: "Do you want to know the sex?"

"Yes," we said in unison. We had made the decision as we pulled into the parking lot.

"I'd give you about a 95 percent chance that it will be a boy."

I was watching the screen from behind her, and I thought it was pretty obvious.

"You can't always be certain because of the angle of the lens and the graininess of the monitor," she added. Dr. Trivedi continued scanning upward, stopping every few seconds to freeze the frame. She measured many of the baby's vital organs and printed pictures of them for the records. Twenty years of delivering babies made the process second nature for the doctor. She continued telling us what she saw as she shifted on her stool to get a picture of the baby's skull.

Suddenly an eerie silence fell upon the room. For several minutes, the only audible sound was the whirring of the monitor and our muted breathing. Nobody had to explain to us that something was not right. I strained to see what she was investigating. The screen showed what looked like the top of a baby's head, only both sides had collapsed, leaving an outline shaped like a lemon. It was obviously very different from any ultrasound picture we had ever seen.

"What does it mean?" I blurted out.

Another silent minute passed with only the whirring of the machines. Then Dr. Trivedi said quietly, "I want you to get a second opinion." As much as we pressed for speculation, all Dr. Trivedi would say was that we should get this opinion soon. She gave us the name and number of a radiologist at the University of Washington.

There, in a sterile hospital room, we learned that our second child would be born with spina bifida, Arnold-Chiari Malformation, and hydrocephalus. As we sat across from specialists at Children's Hospital, the full impact of what this meant hit us like a sledgehammer.

Spina bifida is a defect in which the spinal column does not close around the spinal cord. The severity can range from one vertebra to a majority of the cord being exposed. This means that the spinal cord is unprotected until the baby is born and surgery can be performed: The lack of protection causes serious and permanent damage to this vital nerve center. Just a few decades ago, most children affected by this condition did not live beyond infancy. While modern medical technology has dramatically improved the chances that these children will survive, most are confined to wheelchairs.

Arnold-Chiari Malformation often accompanies spina bifida. The strained spinal cord pulls the brain to the back of the skull and down the spinal column. Hydrocephalus is a technical term for water on the brain. The altered development of the central nervous system causes fluids to accumulate in cavities around the brain called ventricles. The ventricles then push out the skull, enlarging the head. Unchecked, this condition is fatal.

In the original photographs, one-third of our child's brain was not visible to the doctors who analyzed the ultrasounds. They immediately warned us that our baby might not survive the remaining four months to his due date. Any of the three conditions was enough to kill him; together, they created a volatile mix of devastating physical and mental impairments.

We went home and wandered around the house in a state of shock. Once the numbing sensation wore off, we began researching literature to learn what to expect during the stages of our son's development. While the information was helpful, it did not answer some of the deeper questions that haunted me.

Why would God allow this? If He is really in control, then why didn't He prevent this from happening? What does the Bible have to say about our unborn son? Are there stories in the Scriptures about children with severe illnesses? Knowing that a child will have to endure indescribable suffering, why would we want to allow a child to enter this world? Would Karen and I have the strength to bear the consequences of bringing an impaired child into our lives?

Pam Vredevelt

I logged on my computer and went to a Web site that contained the entire Old and New Testaments. From there, I could look up any word or phrase in several different versions. I typed in "spina bifida." No matches. "Birth defects." No matches. Finally, I typed in "birth." There it was: "As [Jesus] passed by, He saw a man blind from birth" (John 9:1, NASB). A birth defect in the Bible.

Not only did Jesus notice the man's condition, but His disciples had the courage to ask Him the reason for it. The passage continued, "And His disciples asked Him, 'Rabbi, who sinned, this man or his parents, that he would be born blind?'" (v. 2)

Jesus responded, "It was neither that this man sinned, nor his parents; but it was so that the works of God might be displayed in him" (v. 3).

The works of God? I was still confused. A footnote explained that a more literal translation of that phrase would be "the glory of God."

How could a crippling illness display God's glory? How would being confined to a wheelchair for life reveal His work? No logical answers came to mind.

If my son were to find a cure for some form of cancer or AIDS, multiple sclerosis, or even spina bifida and give God full credit, that would make sense. If he figured out a way to restructure the world food distribution systems to relieve hunger...if he moved people with an incredible gift of music...if he led a state or a nation to a higher level of moral consciousness...then I could see how God would be glorified.

But to have his head grow unbalanced to the point that his brain would swell and ultimately kill itself; to have his spinal cord exposed and unprotected for nine months, open to a barrage of blows with every bodily movement—that didn't make any sense. I didn't buy it.

I would have to wait several days to get my answer. The following week my wife, daughter, and I made a pilgrimage to my hometown to celebrate Christmas. The break was a welcome reprieve from ongoing visits to the doctor sandwiched into the normal work routine.

I loved visiting that small farming community. It seemed a world away from the hustle and bustle of the city—bumper-to-bumper traffic, noise, and smog. There, amidst the patchwork of green fields surrounding the dairies, a peace descended on me, stilling my restless agitation and leaving my mind as clear as the azure skies above.

On Sunday morning, the entire town shut down so everyone could attend his or her favorite place of worship. This weekend was no exception. My family went to a medium-sized church in the middle of town. We had been members there since I was two years old. The church had a full-time minister, a part-time secretary, and a custodian. We had a choir, Sunday school, youth group, and in more recent years, a bell choir. Each Christmas, the church put on a full musical extravaganza. Though many congregations had chosen in the last few decades to modernize, our traditions had stayed pretty much intact.

As the organ played, my wife and I slipped into a pew about a third of the way down the aisle. I pulled out the ancient hymnbook, even though the song was one of the old tunes that I had sung a million times before. As I began to sing, I heard her voice behind me—the same voice I had heard ever since I was a small child.

Our lives were tied together even before birth. In the cool of the evening, our mothers had taken walks together, each clasping their hands under the child she was carrying. They talked of their families and their dreams.

We were born two weeks apart. My mother had a boy; her friend had a girl. My hair was blond; her hair was red. I had forty-six chromosomes; she had forty-seven. Within a week after we were born, it became apparent that Lindsey had Down's syndrome. My mother was the older of the two moms, in the higher-risk category. Statistics and probabilities would argue that our fates should have been reversed.

Karen and I held our wedding reception in my hometown, and Lindsey was there with her family. She ran over and planted a big kiss on my cheek. We walked arm in arm as more guests arrived. She was in her glory, standing next to the groom. Seeing the radiant glow on her face reminded me of the many times Lindsey's untainted sense of joy had stopped me in my tracks. It seemed to bubble forth from her like a fine champagne that had been shaken before the bottle was uncorked.

And my oh my, could Lindsey sing! Although she could remember only a few tunes, the songs she knew were her all-time favorites. And no one—I mean no one—could match her fervor and zeal. Even when the entire congregation, choir, and instrumentalists pulled out all the stops, you could still hear her voice above them all. Although her words were unclear and she typically finished singing a second or so after the rest of us, none of that mattered. Her heart was right, and everyone loved her for it.

My mind wandered from the hymn we were singing. *Could anything bring more glory to God? Could the practiced trumpets, the trained singers, and the choir's melodies together match Lindsey's tribute of praise?*

The answer to the question I had asked a few days before was right in front of me—actually, right behind me—and I couldn't miss it.

I remembered the church services during my childhood when I used to tip my head back in the pew and visualize myself above the congregation, hovering in the rafters from a vantage point that simulated God's perspective. I'm sure that He found pleasure in the trumpet's tunes, though I have a hunch that a couple of the instrumentalists were more concerned with hitting those last two high notes than whether He was praised. And the choir was marvelous, though I know that a couple of the sopranos held a grudge against the director for not having picked them for solos. Then one year there was a tenor who thought he was a little better than the rest of the guys, and an alto who came to practice mostly to get in on the latest church gossip. But none of these things encumbered sweet Lindsey. She sang each song unabashedly and without pretense, boldly declaring her adoration to the Lord.

> O come, let us adore Him
> > O come, let us adore Him
> O come, let us adore Him,
> > Christ the Lord.

After the service, I walked out of the church into the crisp winter air and strolled down the neatly swept sidewalk to admire the holly wreaths and colored lights decorating the surrounding houses. Gazing into the overcast sky, I realized that God was going to work in our family in a very different way than I had ever imagined. He wanted me to trust Him—Christ the Lord.

Almost twenty-four months have passed since that evening in our little country church. At the moment, I am watching Austin Phillip turn the pages of a colorful picture book as he stands against the couch. His eyes beam such a brilliant blue that everything else looks dull. His frequent bursts of laughter are so contagious that even total strangers spontaneously join in. And although he still needs to hold on, walking is one of his favorite things to do. It is only a matter of time before he will let go of our hands and take off down the hallway.

I shouldn't be surprised. Throughout his development, Austin has defied all odds. While there was a 90 percent chance that his eyesight would be impaired, tests show no abnormalities. He can move both ankles in all directions, a feat almost unheard of in a child whose spinal cord developed outside of his body for several months. Recently, we've even observed some movement in the extremities—those ten little toes that Dr. Trivedi photographed almost two years ago. I know that Austin should be disciplined for kicking his sister, but I have to smile a little when I see him do it—just because he can!

Much to our and our doctors' astonishment, Austin's mental capacity appears to be virtually unaffected by the conditions diagnosed while he was in utero. Like that of any other eighteen-month-old, his vocabulary grows daily. He picks up things from our adult conversation when we aren't even aware that he's listening.

I now know that nothing is impossible with God. Any challenge I face on a day-to-day basis pales in comparison to receiving the news in that radiologist lab at the University of Washington. Little things that used to make me worry now don't.

Today, I also realize that sometimes God uses a different road than we expect to get us where we need to be. When He says, "Trust Me," I have only to look back on the past two years and say, "Okay."

As I've watched this miracle unfold, I have seen first-hand the work of God—in Austin, and in me. And my life will never be the same.

Sometimes we are called upon to endure enormous hard-ship—the loss of a child, a lingering or crippling illness, a financial collapse, the end of a relationship, an unending string of problems, an inexplicable series of tragedies—while those around us appear to be exempt from trouble. At times like these, as we grope for answers, our faith may falter. Our questions may rage toward heaven. But as we grope, seek, face our difficulties square on, and endure, new meaning and growth come. I love what Dr. Scott Peck wrote:

> Problems call forth our courage and our wisdom; indeed they create our courage and our wisdom. It is only because of problems that we grow mentally and spiritually. It is through the pain of confronting and resolving problems that we learn. As Benjamin Franklin said, "Those things that hurt, instruct."
>
> Fearing the pain involved, almost all of us attempt to avoid problems. We procrastinate, forget them, pretend they do not exist. We even take drugs to assist us in ignoring them, so that by deadening ourselves to the pain we can forget the problems that cause the pain. This tendency to avoid problems and

the emotional suffering inherent in them is the primary basis of all mental illness.[1]

But the ones who come out strong and healthy are...

• those who endure pain rather than run from it;
• those who seek the Lord for wisdom rather than denying a problem exists;
• those who look to God for strength rather than trying to muscle through on their own;
• those who face and embrace their pain rather than pretending it isn't there;
• those who ask for divine perspective rather than drawing conclusions based on their own limited understanding.

Those are the ones whose faith becomes the defining characteristic of their lives.

So what challenges are on your horizon today? What tough questions keep surfacing in your thoughts? May I encourage you to face those issues head on and invite God into the process? When you partner with Him, you're sure to discover some life-changing answers to your questions and concrete solutions to your problems along the way. Like David and Karen, you will find Him worthy of adoration.

After all, He is still Christ the Lord.

Power Perks: A Sip of Hope and Humor

Faith is not anti-intellectual. It is an act of man that reaches beyond the limits of our five senses.

Billy Graham

Faith sees the invisible, believes the unbelievable, and receives the impossible.

Corrie ten Boom

There were eleven people, ten men and one woman, hanging on a rope dangling from a helicopter. The weight of eleven people was clearly too much for the rope, so the group decided that one person would have to get off. No one could decide who should go.

Finally the woman volunteered. She gave a touching speech, saying that she would give her life to save the others because women were used to giving up things for their husbands and children. When she finished speaking, all the men started clapping....

Never underestimate the power of a woman.

Never be afraid to try something new.

Remember that amateurs built the ark.

Professionals built the *Titanic*.

Power Perks: A Sip of Hope and Humor

Whatever I have, wherever I am, I can make it through anything in the One who makes me who I am.

> Philippians 4:13, *The Message*

Pile your troubles on GOD's shoulders—
he'll carry your load, he'll help you out.

> Psalm 55:22, *The Message*

Jesus said, "Here's what I want you to do: Find a quiet, secluded place so you won't be tempted to role-play before God. Just be there as simply and honestly as you can manage. The focus will shift from you to God, and you will begin to sense his grace."

> Matthew 6:6, *The Message*

CHAPTER 9

April Fools

A cheerful heart is good medicine.

Proverbs 17:22

Have you ever wondered how doctors maintain their sanity in the midst of the grueling demands of medical practice? Day in and day out they diagnose, advise, and listen to hundreds of sick and needy patients. Remember now: People who are ill usually aren't in the best of moods!

Then, at the end of the day, after the last patient has gone home, there is the pile of paperwork that can look like the Leaning Tower of Pisa. And don't forget the phone calls during the wee hours of the morning. How do medical professionals replenish their energy reserves and refresh their souls? How do they ease the stress associated with the tremendous responsibility of life-and-death decisions? Dr. Knopf answers this question with a story that will tickle your funny bone.

—◦◦◦—

During his spring break from high school, my son, Eric, entered the National Indoor Championship four-wheeler races at the King Dome in Seattle, Washington. On opening day we went to the stadium armed with the video camera to capture on tape the upcoming moments of a lifetime. Eric's best friend was along for fun and to offer technical advice during the taping.

On the second round of practice runs, Eric made a beautiful clean sweep over a jump but landed with a jarring jolt. He was obviously in pain as he tried to pull off to the side of the track. I quickly made my way through the stands and met him in the ambulance, where medical personnel were assessing his injury. The swelling in his wrist was a pretty clear sign that something was broken. So, with his arm in a splint and pain pills in effect, we headed back home, where X rays confirmed my fears. Three weeks in a cast was the prescribed intervention.

Make no mistake: This was not a calamity. When you're in high school, a cast is a badge of courage that has the magnetic power to draw sympathy from girls. Eric decided to milk it to the max. Tongue in cheek, he mused, "If a wrist cast can muster this much attention, just think what a leg cast could deliver!"

The night before April Fools' Day, Eric and his friend asked me to assist them in a prank by applying a leg cast to each of them. They planned to hobble off to school with some wild, hair-raising story about the great tragedy they had survived. Then they'd solicit classmates to write words of encouragement on their casts. At the end of the day, the plan was to cut the messages out of the plaster, and hand-deliver the cast fragments back to their original sources with an April Fools' message the next morning.

It seemed like a harmless joke, so I played along. At ten o'clock we went to the clinic, where I wrapped their legs with packing material and carefully applied the fiber-glass casts. As I was working on the boys, I glanced off to the side and noticed that the medical records that had been sitting on my desk, awaiting my attention, were now stacked neatly in the corner of the office we were in. I was planning to write some time-sensitive reports for these files the following morning before I filed them in their proper place. I soon realized that I had inadvertently stumbled upon an April Fools' prank that someone was planning to play on me. Someone was setting me up to panic over missing files when I sat down at a clean, empty desk the next morning. When a doctor can't find his files, it's serious business.

The opportunity was too good to pass up. Mark, the custodian, also happened to be at the clinic late that night. He became my accomplice. I asked him to hide the charts in a safe place under lock and key in the janitorial room and to write the following note:

Dear Staff,
 I found a bunch of old papers in room 6. I got rid of them for you.
 Mark

The next morning early meetings at the hospital delayed my arrival at the clinic until 8:30 A.M. The rest of the staff members had arrived at their usual time, 7:45. Someone reported the scenario to me later: The nurse practitioner, who was the scheming ringleader, strutted into the front office bragging about the great April Fools' joke she was playing on Dr. Knopf. She said, "Yesterday, before I went home, I hid all the charts that were on his desk. Tee-hee-hee…"

"You're in big trouble!" came the angry reply from the receptionist. "The janitor thought those charts were trash and threw them out!"

The nurse froze in place, horrified by the news. Two seconds later she bolted out the door, sprinted for the dumpster in the back parking lot, threw open the lid, and hopped in. There she was, in her white uniform, clawing and thrashing through the garbage, pitching papers left and right in a frantic effort to find the tossed files.

Meanwhile the front office supervisor was on the phone with the garbage dispatcher insisting that *all* of the garbage truck drivers be paged and ordered back to our office! The whole place was in an uproar.

In a last-ditch effort to locate the files, the reception-ist called Mark, the custodian, awakening him from a deep sleep. She wanted to know *where* in the dumpster he had pitched the files. Were they on the left or right side? In the front, or toward the back? They were desperate for clues.

Being a kindhearted soul, Mark couldn't let them suffer any longer. After a brief pause and a hearty laugh, he told them that the files were hidden in the janitor's supply room. I wish I had a snapshot of the moment my nurse (who was knee-deep in the dumpster) learned where the files were.

I walked into my office that morning to discover my charts stacked in haphazard disarray on my desk, with a big yellow ribbon and note attached: "You are in big trouble! Take care of these charts yourself!"

Eric walked into his school the next morning, doling out pieces of plaster to the kids he had hoodwinked into signing sympathy notes on his cast. If there is a playful prank gene, it is my professional opinion that Eric and I are both carriers.

I agree with Chuck Swindoll: I think it's every bit as rever-ent to laugh as it is to pray. It's good for the mind, body, and spirit. I have a hunch that when we get to heaven, one of the first sounds we'll hear is a melodious chorus of laughter. There will be nothing present to interrupt our giggles, chuckles, snickers, and snorts. Oh, we have so much to look forward to. But for now, let's give life our best shot. Let's fill our thirsty souls by draining every drop of joy out of every day that passes.

Power Perks: A SIP OF HOPE AND HUMOR

Training Courses Now Available for Men:

- Introduction to Common Household Objects I: The Mop
- Introduction to Common Household Objects II: The Sponge
- Dressing Up: Beyond the Funeral and the Wedding
- Refrigerator Forensics: Identifying and Removing the Dead
- Accepting Loss I: If It's Empty, You Can Throw It Away
- Accepting Loss II: If the Milk Expired Three Weeks Ago, Keeping It in the Refrigerator Won't Bring It Back
- Going to the Supermarket: It's Not Just for Women Anymore!
- Recycling Skills I: Boxes That the Electronics Came In
- Recycling Skills II: Styrofoam That Came in the Boxes That the Electronics Came In
- Bathroom Etiquette I: How to Remove Beard Clippings from the Sink
- Bathroom Etiquette II: Let's Wash Those Towels!
- Bathroom Etiquette III: Five Easy Ways to Tell When You're About to Run Out of Toilet Paper

Power Perks: A SIP OF HOPE AND HUMOR

- Giving Back to the Community: How to Donate Fifteen-Year-Old Levis to Goodwill
- Strange but True: She Really May *Not* Care What "Fourth Down and Ten" Means
- Expand Your Entertainment Options: Renting Movies That Don't Fall under the "Action/Adventure" Category
- Yours, Mine, and Ours: Sharing the Remote
- "I Could Have Played a Better Game than That": Why Women Laugh
- "I Don't Know": Be the First Man to Say It!
- The Gas Gauge in Your Car: Sometimes Empty *Means* Empty
- Directions: It's Okay to Ask for Them
- Listening: It's Not Just Something You Do during Halftime
- Accepting Your Limitations: Just Because You Have Power Tools Doesn't Mean You Can Fix It

For Sale by Owner: Complete set of encyclopedias. Excellent condition. $1,000 or best offer. No longer needed. Got married last weekend. Wife knows everything.

CHAPTER 10

An Angel behind Every Desk

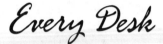

praise you Father, Lord of heaven and earth, because you have hidden these things from the wise and learned, and revealed them to little children."

Matthew 11:25

Remember your favorite teacher when you were growing up? My guess is that he or she probably had some things in common with Mrs. Hannon, the teacher you're about to meet. She's the kind of woman who really—I mean *really*—loves kids and wants to make a difference in their lives.

We all know that teachers, just like everyone else, sometimes have bad days. But Mrs. Hannon wasn't just having a bad day; she was having a string of bad weeks—that is until little Andrew whispered something in her ear that caught her completely by surprise and gave her a fresh outlook on life.

In addition to being a wife and mother, I teach third- and fourth-grade students at a public grade school. I suppose that the children in my class are like those in the average classroom across the country. On many occasions, I have marveled at their resiliency.

The majority of the children in my class have weathered the challenges of divorce. Some live with single parents; others live in blended families or reside with a close relative. Three of my students have parents in prison or on parole. Two have parents in drug rehabilitation. Other children have been neglected and abused. One child, currently caught in the middle of a vicious custody battle, isn't allowed to see her mother. Another lost his father last year in an industrial accident, while yet another lost hers to AIDS. Several in the class struggle with learning disabilities.

Each fall before the school year begins, my husband and I visit my empty classroom and pray for the students who will soon walk through the door. We stroll up and down the aisles, praying over each desk, asking the Lord to place His angels around the children who will occupy the seats. We ask Him to protect, help, and watch over them with love.

Partway through this school year I was ending a long,

tough month. Generally I handle stress well, but I was exhausted from the ongoing strain of burdens we were bearing. In addition to the challenges in the classroom, my husband's ninety-one-year-old father became very ill while visiting our home. When the doctor examined him, we discovered that he had a pancreatic tumor, which required surgery. Wanting to help, my husband and I admitted him to the local hospital in town. The surgery went well, but when he was transferred to a nursing facility for additional therapy, he contracted pneumonia, and the doctors didn't know if he would survive.

While my husband spent countless hours at the nursing home, I picked up his load and mine on the home front: the meals, the taxi service for our daughter, the daily chores—all the things you have to do to keep a household running. We were also providing shelter for a friend and her baby. She was separated from her abusive husband. They were receiving counseling and hoping for reconciliation.

You might say my plate was full—so full that it was beginning to crack.

About the time I hit an all-time low, my friend's husband did not show up for a counseling session as expected. Instead, he served her divorce papers, forcibly took their nursing child from her, and disappeared. We had no idea where to find him. Although she had legal custody and a court order, the police could not locate the man to rescue her son. It was psychological torment.

When Monday morning arrived, I didn't think I would be able to pull myself together to face my class. Most of my energy had gone swirling down the drain. My job typically requires 100 percent, and I felt like I had about 2 percent to offer. But I pushed myself to go and managed to squeak through the door just as the bell was about to ring.

That morning, I worked with the children in the computer lab on a project we called "All about Me." Their assignment was to write a story about what they wanted to be when they grew up. In the middle of the exercise, Andrew called me over to his computer and asked, "Mrs. Hannon, how do you spell *mighty?*"

After spelling it out for him, I asked him how he was using the word.

"When I grow up, I want to be a mighty man of God," he replied.

"Wow—what a wonderful ambition, Andrew!" I said.

Andrew's comment sparked interest in Mitchell, who was sitting at the computer next to him. He turned to Andrew and asked, "What's a mighty man of God?"

Curious to hear what Andrew would say, I listened carefully.

"It's like being a warrior for God—someone who wears God's armor."

Andrew motioned to me with his index finger to come

closer. He wanted to whisper something in my ear. When I was close enough, he said softly, "Mrs. Hannon, do you believe in angels?"

"Yes, Andrew, as a matter of fact, I do."

"But Mrs. Hannon, do you believe people can see angels?"

I whispered back, "Well, angels appeared to the shepherds and told them that Jesus had been born. And there are many other stories in the Bible that speak of people seeing angels. I believe that if God wants people to see angels, they'll see them."

He then asked me to come even closer, so that no one else could hear. Very softly he said, "Mrs. Hannon, I see an angel."

"Andrew, are you telling me that right now—at this very moment—you see an angel?" I whispered in astonishment.

Looking up at me with a twinkle in his eye and grinning from ear to ear, he said, "No, Mrs. Hannon, I don't see one angel. I see lots and lots of angels. There is one standing right behind every kid's desk."

I smiled, nodded affirmatively, and said, "I believe you, Andrew." Though I couldn't see the angels like Andrew did, I reveled in the magnificence of God's power and love standing guard over each one in my class. The message was crystal clear. God was carefully attending to all the needs represented, including my own. He *did* answer prayer. He *did* respond to deep concern. He *was* present when he seemed most absent.

In time, my father-in-law recovered fully and returned to Arizona in good health. The police found the stolen baby and returned him to his mother. She and her son are now living in the safety of a shelter, awaiting a court hearing.

And Andrew—well, I think he's making great strides toward his goal.

Power Perks: A Sip of Hope and Humor

He ordered his angels
>   to guard you wherever you go.
If you stumble, they'll catch you;
>   their job is to keep you from falling….
"If you'll hold on to me for dear life," says GOD,
>   "I'll get you out of any trouble.
I'll give you the best of care
>   if you'll only get to know and trust me.
Call me and I'll answer, be at your side in bad times;
>   I'll rescue you, then throw you a party.
I'll give you a long life,
>   and give you a long drink of salvation!"

Psalm 91:11–12, 14–16, *The Message*

An ordinary night with ordinary sheep and ordinary shepherds. And were it not for a God who loves to hook an "extra" on the front of the ordinary, the night would have gone unnoticed. The sheep would have been forgotten, and the shepherds would have slept the night away.

But God dances amidst the common. And that night he did a waltz.

Power Perks: A Sip of Hope and Humor

The black sky exploded with brightness…. Sheep that had been silent became a chorus of curiosity. One minute the shepherd was dead asleep, the next he was rubbing his eyes and staring into the face of an alien.

The night was ordinary no more.

The angel came in the night because that is when lights are best seen and that is when they are most needed. God comes into the common for the same reason.

Max Lucado[1]

Christians should never fail to sense the operation of angelic glory. It forever eclipses the world of demonic powers, as the sun does a candle's light.

Billy Graham

The angel of the LORD encamps around those who fear Him, and rescues them. O taste and see that the LORD is good. How blessed is the man who takes refuge in Him!

Psalm 34:7–8, NASB

CHAPTER 11
Gentle Invitations

A little child will lead them.

Isaiah 11:6

Do you wonder sometimes at the ways God gets our attention? He knows what each of us needs and provides the perfect impetus to invite our prayers. In the course of everyday life with my handicapped son, I find many moments when I am able to hear God's gentle invitation to talk with Him.

It happened today. We were in Nathan's bedroom, picking up toys together, when he suddenly dropped the puzzle he was holding. The sharp corner of the cardboard struck the tender skin on the top of his foot. Immediately Nathan burst into tears, fell to the ground, and held his foot, wailing, "Ooowwweeee!"

I tried to pat his back and hug him, but he was too focused on the pain to receive my comfort. Brushing my hand away from his shoulder, he clasped his hands together and held them up in my face. Using sign language, he was asking me to pray for him.

The moment I laid my hand on his foot and started praying, Nathan grew quiet. I prayed simple words in short sentences. As I spoke, he tried his best to mimic what I was saying to the Lord. They were broken syllables—awkward attempts at consonants. Nathan's language was unintelligible to the average human ear. But God knew his heart. And Nathan's words were sweet melodies to His ears.

Nathan is usually the first one to ask to pray when we sit down for a family dinner. Clasping his hands and holding them up high for all of us to see, he enthusiastically claims his place in the lineup. And when he prays, it's quite heartwarming. With his eyes wide open he looks at each person, mutters a stream of garbled sounds, and works his way slowly around the circle until he has talked to the Lord about each one present. Then he prays for Kelli, Shawn, and Tia, some of his closest friends. I'm a bit embarrassed to admit it, but there have been times when the rest of us have been chomping at the bit for him to finish his long-winded prayers so that we could eat before our food got cold.

I noticed his sensitivity to prayer when he was very small. One afternoon when was about three years old, he ran through the living room, tripped over his floppy feet, and went flying into the corner of the coffee table. Hiding his face in his hands, he screamed at the top of his lungs. When

I picked him up to help, he was covered with blood flowing from a deep gash over his right eye. He was so distraught that my efforts to calm him were completely unsuccessful. So I prayed. "Dear God, please touch Nathan," I began.

The moment I started praying Nathan stopped screaming and sat quietly on my lap. I finished the prayer, washed his wound, and applied antibiotic cream, all with his complete cooperation. The dramatic change in him spoke volumes to me about the mystery of God's presence in this little boy's life. Though he is mentally retarded, he is spiritually perceptive.

We saw evidence of this again when he was four years old. Our family spent Memorial Day weekend camping on the Deschutes River in Eastern Oregon. We had a wonderful time until the drive home, when we ended up in stop-and-go traffic on the highway from Bend to Portland. Our usual three-hour scenic trip turned into a five-and-a-half-hour endurance marathon.

We had taken two vehicles that weekend. Nathan and I were in the car following my husband, John, and our other kids, Jessie and Ben, who were in our camper. Jessie and Ben snoozed their way through the congestion while John tried to keep his mind on more positive things than the bumper in front of him. After an hour and twenty minutes of creeping along at ten miles an hour, the traffic finally cleared, and our speedometers hit fifty-five again.

Nathan was quiet most of the trip. He surprised me

when he suddenly broke the silence with "Mama, Mama!" while clasping his hands in front of him.

"All right, Nathan," I said, "who do you want me to pray for?"

"Nnnn," came the reply.

That's Nathan's word for Andrew, the little boy up the street who plays with Ben now and then. So I prayed for Andrew. I asked God to bless him and his family.

Then Nathan clasped his hands again and asked me to pray for Jessie. Then Ben. Then Dad. Then Mama. Then Grandma and Grandpa. After praying at length for the entire family, I figured we were done. Not according to Nathan! My little copilot kept giving me the "pray" sign while adamantly pointing to our camper in front of us.

"Nathan," I explained, "Mommy *already* prayed for Daddy and Jessie and Ben."

Irritated, he again gave me the "pray" sign and pointed to the camper.

What in the world did he want? What was on his heart? I could tell that he felt very strongly about what he was trying to communicate. So I made some guesses. "Nathan, do you want me to pray for Daddy?"

"No."

"Jessie?"

"No."

"Ben?"

"No."

He kept pointing to the camper. Insistently. I gave it one more try. "Nathan, do you want me to pray for the camper?"

"Da!" (Nathan's version of yes.)

I thought the request a bit strange, but I accommodated him and prayed that God would take care of the camper and keep it in good working condition all the way home. After I said amen, Nathan relaxed. He seemed happy, and that was that.

A few breaths later, though, we rounded a curve, crested a hill, and had to slam on our brakes as our camper suddenly skidded wildly to a stop in front of us. John and I had happened upon an accident that had just occurred. A truck pulling a large horse trailer had crashed into a motor home that stopped abruptly for another car crossing its lane. The force of the impact had lifted the rear of the motor home off the ground and spun it around, leaving it in the lane of oncoming traffic. The right front wheel had popped off and the motor home was tilted to the side. Smoke rolled across the highway in clouds. Injured passengers scrambled out of damaged vehicles to get out of danger.

The people in the car in front of us pulled flares from their trunks, dialed their cell phones, checked the injured, and directed traffic.

I just sat there, stunned. I couldn't believe what I was seeing. It so easily could have been us—our whole family! Minutes before, John and I had been the ones in front of the truck pulling the horses.

I'm not sure I understand the connection between Nathan's insistence that I pray specifically for the camper and our protection on the road that day. But I do believe there was a connection.

Nathan is now eight years old. Last night when I put him to bed, we did what we always do. I told him a story and then laid down next to him to review the day. He clasped his little hands and held them in front of his face, inviting me to pray. We joined all four hands together and closed off the evening with God. One simple word at a time. I led. And he followed along to the best of his ability. They were sweet, peaceful moments after a very active day.

Nathan dozed off into dreamland, and I lingered a while longer, not wanting to disturb the calm. The expression on Nathan's face spoke of contentment. As I laid quietly beside him, gently holding his hands, I reflected over the years Nathan has been with us. I thought of the many lessons this fragile child has taught me. But one seemed prominent at the moment: *He has led me closer to the heart of God.*

Nathan's handicaps remind me of the harsh realities and the permanent suffering inherent in this world. But his promptings to pray remind me where to go for relief. Peace and comfort are found in God's presence, and Nathan finds delight in leading me there. If you were to meet him, he'd ask you to come too.

Please consider yourself invited.

Power Perks: A Sip of Hope and Humor

And what kind of habitation pleases God? What must our natures be like for him to feel at home within us? He asks nothing, but a pure heart and a single mind. He asks no rich paneling, not rugs from the Orient, no art treasures from afar. He desires but sincerity, transparency, humility, and love. He will see to the rest.

A. W. Tozer

A pastor wearing clerical clothes was walking along the corridor near the preschool wing of the parochial school when a group of little ones trotted by on the way to the cafeteria. One little lad of about three or four stopped, looked at his clothes, and asked, "Why do you dress funny?"

The man told the lad that he was a pastor and this was the uniform that pastors wore.

Then the boy pointed to the pastor's collar and asked, "Do you have an owie?"

The pastor was perplexed until he realized that to the boy the collar looked like a bandage. So the pastor took it out and handed it to the boy. On the back were raised letters giving the name of the manufacturer.

Power Perks: A Sip of Hope and Humor

The little guy felt the letters, and the pastor asked, "Do you know what those words say?"

"Yes, I do," said the lad, who was not old enough to read. Peering intently at the letters, he said, "Kills ticks and fleas up to six months!"

To be brought within the zone of God's voice is to be profoundly altered.

Oswald Chambers

Don't fret or worry. Instead of worrying, pray. Let petitions and praises shape your worries into prayers, letting God know your concerns. Before you know it, a sense of God's wholeness, everything coming together for good, will come and settle you down. It's wonderful what happens when Christ displaces worry at the center of your life.

Philippians 4:6–7, *The Message*

CHAPTER 12

The Mile-Wide Space in the Middle of the Bed

*D*on't grieve God. Don't break his heart. His Holy Spirit, moving and breathing in you, is the most intimate part of your life, making you fit for himself. Don't take such a gift for granted. Make a clean break with all cutting, backbiting, profane talk. Be gentle with one another, sensitive. Forgive one another as quickly and thoroughly as God in Christ forgave you.

Ephesians 4:30–32, *The Message*

I started the day in a slump. Dragging myself out of bed, I read my Bible with little enthusiasm while sipping a steaming cup of French vanilla coffee. I think someone at the store must have played a dirty trick by putting decaf in the regular coffee bin, because thirty minutes later I still felt like a slug on the front walk, unwilling to move. What to do when even coffee doesn't help jump-start my initiative?

Well, I fixed breakfast for the kids, kissed their cheeks, shooed them off to their first day of school, and sat down at my computer to write. Nothing came. Zip. Zilch. Blank screen.

A grievous gloom settled.

I knew my reserves were somewhat depleted from an active summer with the family. Besides that, getting organized for a new school year always adds more stress to my life. There is simply more to do: school supplies and clothes shopping, haircuts, sports team tryouts, piles of forms to complete, and checks to write. I know it's the same stuff every other mom in America has to do. I suppose I had an extra measure of anxiety because two of my children were going to new schools, and the third had a new principal. I was hoping and praying that the transitions would be positive.

"What I need is some fresh air and blood in my brain," I muttered. So I opened the window, allowing a fifty-five-degree breeze to chill my office. I figured that some physical movement might also help, so I threw a load of towels in the wash, folded and put away some clean clothes upstairs, and warmed my coffee in the microwave.

Twenty minutes later, I tried again.

Oh, well.

Lord, I don't know what's the matter with me, but I'm just not myself. I'm sure there is something You'd like to say through me, but I don't have a clue what it is. Please God, speak to me and lead me by Your Spirit today, I prayed.

I sat in silence for a while, asking God to help me focus my attention on what He wanted me to be mindful of at the moment. Clarity began to come.

I was angry. My husband and I had had an argument the night before, and I was having a hard time letting go of the ill feelings it had triggered. It was a petty thing. We were scheduled to shoot a video series for married couples on a particular date. He was certain that he had told me the date, but I was sure that he hadn't. I had told him that an out-of-town guest was coming that weekend and that he had entered his reminder on a different weekend. So now we had to reschedule the video shoot, which was embarrassing for both of us and an inconvenience to the people involved. Neither of us was happy with the other. Someone could have parked a truck in the middle of our king-size bed that night, and we would have never known it. We were both hugging the edges.

Silly, isn't it? Two educated adults, who teach couples how to achieve intimacy in their marriages, end up in a standoff about a scheduling mix-up. Oh, we both had our rational arguments. But I didn't want to hear his, and he didn't want to hear mine. And make no mistake: This time, I wanted him to be the first to say that he was sorry. As far as I was concerned, he had made the bigger error. The Pharisee within me stood tall, refusing to budge an inch.

And the results? Alienation from my partner in life. Flat emotion. Soul fatigue. Stifled creativity. Self-deception. And grief to the Spirit of God.

That's the power of the Pharisee Syndrome. It leads us to believe that we are faultless, or at least less at fault than another. That we know better. That we *are* better. I went back and reread the parable of the Pharisee:

> He [Jesus] told his next story to some who were complacently pleased with themselves over their moral performance and looked down their noses at the common people: "Two men went up to the Temple to pray, one a Pharisee, the other a tax man. The Pharisee posed and prayed like this: 'Oh, God, I thank you that I am not like other people—robbers, crooks, adulterers, or, heaven forbid, like this tax man. I fast twice a week and tithe on all my income.'
>
> "Meanwhile the tax man, slumped in the shadows, his face in his hands, not daring to look up, said, 'God, give mercy. Forgive me, a sinner.'"
>
> Jesus commented, "This tax man, not the other, went home made right with God. If you walk around with your nose in the air, you're going to end up flat on your face, but if you're content to be simply yourself, you will become more than yourself." (Luke 18:9–14, *The Message*)

I sighed and turned to my Father in heaven: *Well, I guess that about hits the nail on the head, Lord. That's how I feel today—like someone who is flat on my face, without much oomph to get up. Okay, I get the message. I forgive John.*

By the way, my feelings were saying the exact opposite, but I knew I needed to choose to forgive anyway. I wanted to be right with God, and I knew that If I didn't respond to what God was showing me, things were not going to get better for me or with John. I sensed the Holy Spirit's sadness over the hardness of our hearts toward each other. God *is* love, and anything that isn't pains Him.

A thought crossed my mind: *It is more important to love than to be right.*

Lord, please forgive me for acting like a Pharisee. I detest how I think and act when I play that role. I don't want to be a person who is stubborn, self-willed, critical, and demanding. I surrender my need to be right to You, and ask You to help John and me make things right between us.

I called John at work and apologized for my part in the conflict. He apologized for his. It wasn't a conversation for a Hallmark commercial. No warm fuzzies were present for either of us. And when I hung up the phone I was amazed at how unrelenting the Pharisee within me was to make a point. I was still secretly hoping that John had grasped the fact that I was right and he was wrong. My oh my, pride dies hard.

I'm so glad that God is bigger than our dark side. I'm

so thankful that I'm not alone in my struggle. I think of the candid words Paul spoke to the Romans about his inner struggles:

> I truly delight in God's commands, but it's pretty obvious that not all of me joins in that delight. Parts of me covertly rebel, and just when I least expect it, they take charge. I've tried everything and nothing helps. I'm at the end of my rope. Is there no one who can do anything for me? Isn't that the real question? (Romans 7:22–24, *The Message*)

> And I find hope in how he responds to the problem: The answer, thank God, is that Jesus Christ can and does. He acted to set things right in this life of contradictions where I want to serve God with all my heart and mind, but am pulled by the influence of sin to do something totally different…. God's Spirit is right alongside helping us along. (Romans 7:25, 8:26, *The Message*)

During my lunch break later that afternoon, I picked up a book I hadn't read from for several weeks. I didn't realize it at the time, but now I see that the Holy Spirit directed my choice. He wasn't finished with me yet.

With a cheese sandwich in hand, I turned to a new chapter in Henri Nouwen's book *The Road to Daybreak.*

Nouwen, a Catholic priest trained at Yale University, held a professorship at Harvard and traveled the world as a renowned author and lecturer. Midway through his career, he left behind prestige and power to serve severely handicapped people in France. This book chronicles his spiritual journey during those years of transition. Portions of one journal entry challenged me to rethink my pious position.

It is hard for me to speak of my feelings of being rejected or imposed upon, of my desire for affirmation as well as my need for space, of insecurity and mistrust, of fear and love. But as I entered into these feelings, I also discovered the real problem—expecting from a friend what only Christ can give....

I learned afresh that friendship requires a constant willingness to forgive each other for not being Christ, and a willingness to ask Christ himself to be the true center. When Christ does not mediate a relationship, that relationship easily becomes demanding, manipulating, oppressive, an arena for many forms of rejection. An unmediated friendship cannot last long; you simply expect too much of the other and cannot offer the other the space he or she needs to grow. Friendship requires closeness, affection, support, and mutual encouragement, but also distance, space to grow, freedom to be different, and solitude. To nurture both aspects of a relationship, we must experience a deeper and more lasting affirmation than any human relationship can offer.... Constant mutual forgiveness and a continual openness to the love of God are the disciplines which allow us to grow together in friendship.[1]

Instead of starting lunch with a prayer, I ended it with one: *Oh, God. I forgive John for not being You. Help me to never stop forgiving and to always remain open to You and Your love. Help John to forgive too. And please enable me to love him the way You love me.*

Just in case you're wondering, the rest of the day wasn't exactly fabulous, but it was a whole lot better. We both made an effort to repair the breach. John realized that he had overreacted, and I realized that I had overreacted to his overreaction. It wasn't a fairy-tale ending, but at least we were on the same page! When we went to sleep that night, the space in the middle of the bed was gone. And so was the Holy Spirit's grief.

Power Perks: A Sip of Hope and Humor

Forgiveness is not an occasional act; it's a permanent attitude.

Martin Luther King Jr.

If God were not willing to forgive sin, heaven would be empty.

German proverb

When you forgive, you in no way change the past, but you sure do change the future.

Bernard Meltzer

The heaviest load any man carries on his back is a pack of grudges.

Peter got up the nerve to ask, "Master, how many times do I forgive a brother or sister who hurts me? Seven?"

Jesus replied, "Seven! Hardly. Try seventy times seven."

Matthew 18:21–22, *The Message*

As we grow in wisdom, we pardon more freely.

Anne Louise Germaine De-Stael

My ability to be an *instrument* of God's grace is limited by my willingness to be an *object* of God's grace. The degree to which I allow my ugliness to be revealed to Him is the degree to which His beauty will be revealed through me.

Dan Chriestenson

CHAPTER 13

Holidaze

A prudent man gives thought to his steps.

Proverbs 14:15

"The holidays are going to be fun this year," I told John, glancing at my December calendar. I was looking forward to the children's Christmas programs and the smell of fresh-cut evergreens and Christmas cookies wafting through the house. Besides that, Christmas break meant a minivacation from my typical 5:30 A.M. reveille on school days. Just thinking about the possibility of sleeping in gave me a boost.

There have been holidays when not much of anything has given me a lift—when it was all I could do to muster up the energy to decorate the tree and wrap a few gifts for John and the kids. During the two years following Nathan's traumatic birth and diagnosis of Down's syndrome, I was plagued with a persistent, low-grade depression. I tried to be positive, but I was still sad. The thought of raising a mentally retarded boy overwhelmed me. Grief is hard work, and it sapped most of my energy, making the holidays a test of endurance instead of a celebration of joy.

But things change over time, and I felt that this year was going to be different. We were more adjusted. Nathan's previous health concerns were no longer an issue, and all three of our children seemed to be adjusting well at school.

"If you'll back the truck out of the garage, I'll get the decorations out of the attic," I told John, handing him the keys. It was Thanksgiving weekend, and I was a woman on a mission: Christmas was coming to the Vredevelt household! After brewing a fresh pot of coffee, I cranked up one of our favorite Christmas CDs and went to work. Who could have known what scary surprise lay in wait for me?

After climbing the attic stairs, I flipped on the light and scanned the boxes, taking inventory of what needed to go inside. The giant wreath went first, followed by the hand-carved Nativity scene and holiday candleholders. Eager to decorate the mantel over our fireplace, I searched for the box labeled "Children's Christmas Stockings." Peering into the dark spaces under the rafters, I squinted, trying to bring into focus the writing on the side of each box.

"Aha! There it is!" I said, spotting the box of stockings wedged behind some other items. Shoving a couple of things out of the way, I reached for the box, but my arms weren't long enough to get a good grip on it. *You have to move in closer,* I told myself.

I took another step toward the box. Then I suddenly found myself falling like a bombshell through the floor of the attic into our garage. Sheetrock went flying everywhere. In the middle of my supersonic descent, I instinctively reached for a couple of rafters on my left and right. There I was, arms hooked on the rafters, dangling in midair in our garage, right smack between two mountain bikes that were hanging from hooks on the ceiling.

If I let go of these rafters, those bike pedals are going to cut me to shreds, I thought. My hip was already in searing pain, and my armpits were collecting splinters.

There was no other option. "Help! Help!" I yelled at the top of my lungs.

Wouldn't you know it—everyone else was inside the house, where the Christmas music was blaring, drowning out my cries for assistance.

Finally, Kelli, a friend who was living with us at the time, heard my screams and opened the door into the garage. She looked left. Nothing. She looked right. Nothing. Bewildered and panicked by the sound of my voice, she frantically yelled, "Where are you? I can't see you!"

"I'm up here!" I yelled. "Hurry!"

When she looked up, a pitiful sight met her eyes: half of a body protruding through a jagged hole in the ceiling of the garage.

"Oh! Oh! I'm coming! I'm coming!" she called frantically. Kelli flew up those steps, and within seconds she had lifted me carefully through the hole to safety.

Leave it to me: I had found the one small section of the attic where the Sheetrock had not been covered with floorboard, and I had stepped on it with my full weight.

Oh, well.

Moments later the rest of the family gathered curiously in a huddle under the mountain bikes, their mouths hanging open, staring at the hole in the ceiling. Never mind that they were more interested in the torn-up ceiling than their banged-up mother!

"Mom, you're supposed to use the stairs," Ben ribbed.

"Pam, you need to walk on the floorboard," John said, shaking his head, utterly bemused by my stunt.

Laughing over the ridiculous turn of events and whimpering over the pain in my hip, I hobbled into the house to examine the battle wounds. Sure enough, there was a blood blister on my left hip the size of a grapefruit. It turned every conceivable shade of purple, blue, black, and green—not a pretty thing. I was glad that it was winter, because swimming was definitely out of the question.

The following week at the counseling center, I moaned about my mishap to my colleagues Steve and Craig.

Being an empathetic therapist, Steve wanted me to know I wasn't the only one who did stupid things like that. "I have a good friend who had a similar mishap," he said.

Dan and Mandy, so he said, were getting ready for out-of-town guests. Mandy's close friend from high school was coming with her husband and children, all the way from Michigan to Oregon for a ten-day visit. At the time, Dan and Mandy's children were preschoolers, so preparing for company was a bit of a challenge. No matter how hard they tried to organize the house, it seemed that there was no end to putting away the toys and kiddie paraphernalia lying around. Mandy had other concerns too.

"Dan, I keep hearing strange sounds in the bathroom ceiling," Mandy reported. "Every now and then the lights flicker. Would you check things out?" She wanted to be sure that they didn't have any uninvited vermin dropping in while her friends were in town.

Dan crawled up into the attic space to explore the odd noises. That was no small task for a strong husky man more than six feet tall. With flashlight in hand, he headed toward the northwest end of the house.

Grateful for his help, Mandy tackled her to-do list and began dusting the living room, which they had converted into sleeping quarters for their friends. She had finished one corner and just moved to the center of the room when *Wham! Bam! Crash!* Dan rocketed through the ceiling, sending particles of Sheetrock flying everywhere. Mandy spun around to behold something too bizarre to be real: Half of Dan was flailing wildly just above her. One leg was hooked over the ceiling beam and the other was flying around like an unguided missile.

Mandy was lucky that Dan's foot didn't crash-land on her face. All this was in full swing (pun intended) when their six-year-old son, Joseph, walked into the living room, stopped abruptly, sized up the situation, put his hands on his hips, and said somberly, "Dad, you broke our house!"

Isn't that the way it goes? You invite company over for a visit, make every effort to put the house in order, and that's about the time the garbage disposal goes *ka-poo-ee* or the toilets back up and the unexpected guest for dinner turns out to be the Roto-Rooter man. It has happened to us on more than one holiday occasion. To this day, I refuse to put potato or onion peelings down the disposal, even though the heavy-duty commercial brand we installed is supposedly capable of eating rocks. If I can, I try to ward off potential problems.

But sometimes there is just no way to prepare for the holiday mishaps that come our way. Just ask my friend Penny.

Penny was nineteen when she accepted a customer service position at the local bookstore. Full of life, she loved working with people and made it her goal to put a smile on the face of every person she served.

Christmas was her favorite time of year in the store. Scented candles flickered softly, and white lights twinkled a warm welcome to customers. Carols playing quietly in the background calmed the agitation of even the most mission-minded shoppers—until December 24. Then things changed. "Peace on earth" was definitely happening somewhere else in the world. As soon as the doors were unlocked, crazed shoppers raced through the store, nearly bulldozing the friendly staff in a wild dash for the last few items on their Christmas lists.

That evening the edge of everyone's nerves had been sanded to a fine point, and the atmosphere needed some real fa-la-la. Penny just happened to be the one to remind everyone that it was, after all, "the season to be jolly."

The store was jam-packed, splitting at the seams with customers. In the middle of helping someone with a book order, Penny needed one of the other employees to research some information on the computer for her. Her coworker was busy with another customer on the phone, so leaning on the counter, Penny patiently waited for a natural break in the conversation to ask for assistance. Dave, another employee, noticed Penny waiting and asked if he could help her. "Sure," she said, stepping away from the counter toward Dave.

But something was amiss. As Penny backed away, the button on her wraparound tea-length skirt got caught between the seams in the counter. Suddenly her skirt fell from her hips and hit the ground, sending a shock wave through the line of customers in view. Seeing the horror on Dave's face, Penny flew into hysterics. Dave immediately covered his eyes with both hands, made an about-face, and ran the other way. Penny's coworker behind the counter lost all semblance of professionalism and started laughing so hard that she had to hang up the phone on a customer because she couldn't breathe.

In a split second a whirlwind of thoughts raced through Penny's mind. *What am I going to do? If I run to the bathroom at the other side of the store more people will see me. Should I get dressed, right here, in front of God and everybody else standing around?*

Logic prevailed. Penny quietly stooped down, picked up her skirt, wrapped it around her waist, fastened the button securely, and pretended that nothing out of the ordinary had just happened.

Just about then a soft tap on her shoulder startled her. With a surge of nervous energy, she spun around and looked into the smiling eyes of a gentleman who had been standing in line through the entire ordeal. "Wow—you girls sure pull out all the stops to sell a book!" he teased.

For the first time in her life, Penny was speechless.

Later that evening, the store manager left her with a few words of wisdom: "Penny, I'm glad that you are an enthusiastic employee, but we do have a policy here. You need to keep your clothes on when you're helping customers!"

Power Perks: A Sip of Hope and Humor

Christmas began in the heart of God. It is complete only when it reaches the heart of man.

Ten Ways to Know If You Have PMS

1. Everyone around you has an attitude problem.
2. You're adding chocolate chips to your cheese omelette.
3. The dryer has shrunk every last pair of your jeans.
4. Your husband is suddenly agreeing with everything you say.
5. You're using your cell phone to respond to every bumper sticker that says, "How's my driving? Call 1-800-xxx-xxxx."
6. Everyone's head looks like an invitation to batting practice.
7. You're convinced that there's a God and He's male.
8. You're counting down the days until menopause.
9. You're sure that everyone is scheming to drive you crazy.
10. The ibuprofen bottle you bought yesterday is empty.

Laughing one hundred times a day works the heart as much as exercising for ten minutes on a rowing machine.

It is Christmas every time you let God love others through you…yes, it is Christmas every time you smile at your brother and offer him your hand.

Mother Teresa of Calcutta

It is often just as sacred to laugh as it is to pray.

Chuck Swindoll

CHAPTER 14

Handyman Horrors

If you don't know what you're doing, pray to the Father. He loves to help. You'll get his help, and won't be condescended to when you ask for it. Ask boldly, believingly, without a second thought.

James 1:5–6, *The Message*

Is your to-do list growing a mile a minute? Are your tasks outrunning your resources? Are you feeling overwhelmed? Too tired or irritated to pray? Too embarrassed to ask for help? May I encourage you to relinquish a sense of self-sufficiency and look to the One who longs for you to boldly approach His throne of grace? Like Marc, I think you'll find the results quite rewarding.

Marc Gale wouldn't call himself a first-rate handyman, but he does his fair share of fix-it jobs around the house. One day, he had been working for nearly a half an hour trying to open a valve on his water heater. None of the normal techniques worked. He had to position the wrench just right and apply just the right amount of pressure. If he pushed too hard and slipped, he would lose every knuckle on his left hand.

It wasn't a fun job. He spent thirty minutes hunched over on his knees, with sweat dripping off his brow onto his glasses. Each unsuccessful attempt to jar the valve loose ignited more frustration. There was enough mounting tension inside Marc to set off a Mount Saint Helen's blast.

Out of sheer exasperation he was just about ready to pitch the wrench when his nine-year-old son, Andrew, rounded the corner. Andrew exuded his usual peaceful attitude toward life and cheerfully asked, "What's up, Dad?"

Marc nearly jumped down Andrew's throat for interrupting his work, but something stopped him. He took a breath, turned to Andrew, and said, "Son, I need you to pray for me."

Without hesitation, without questioning, Andrew walked over to Marc, laid his hand on his shoulder, and prayed, *Dear God, please help my Dad. He is upset and needs Your help with this job. Amen.*

One more gentle push on the wrench and— *whammo*—the valve opened. Marc jumped to his feet, hugged his son, and shouted, *Thank You, God!*

———

Postscript: Andrew has been frequently called in for subsequent home repairs. His prayers have not always brought the same miraculous results, particularly the time the toilet blew up. But Marc's wife, Diana, says that it's good for Andrew to keep on praying. The real miracle is Marc's positive attitude as he deals with the frustrations of his handyman assignments.

Power Perks: A Sip of Hope and Humor

Don't hold back. Throw yourselves into the work of the Master, confident that nothing you do for him is a waste of time or effort.

1 Corinthians 15:58, The Message

Get along among yourselves, each of you doing your part.... Gently encourage the stragglers, and reach out for the exhausted, pulling them to their feet. Be patient with each person, attentive to individual needs.

1 Thessalonians 5:13–14, The Message

Those of us who are strong and able in the faith need to step in and lend a hand to those who falter, and not just do what is most convenient for us. Strength is for service, not status.

Romans 15:1, The Message

Every noble work is at first impossible.

Thomas Carlyle

Little strokes fell great oaks.

Henry Ward Beecher

I heard a story about a little girl who, on the way home from church, turned to her mother and said, "Mommy, the preacher's sermon this morning confused me."

"What was confusing?" the mother asked.

The girl thought for a moment and said, "Well, he said that God is bigger than we are. Is that true?"

"Yes, honey, that's true," the mother replied.

"He also said that God lives within us. Is that true too?"

Again the mother replied, "Yes."

"Well," said the girl, "if God is bigger than us and He lives in us, wouldn't He show through?"

CHAPTER 15

A Miracle in the Third Row

esus] took a little child and had him stand among them. Taking him in his arms, he said to them, "Whoever welcomes one of these little children in my name welcomes me; and whoever welcomes me does not welcome me but the one who sent me."

Mark 9:36–37

Butterflies danced in Charonne's stomach when thirty-three first graders entered her room on the first day of school. One by one they hung up their jackets, took their seats, and peered in her direction. As she scanned the sea of faces, the eyes staring back at her reflected a myriad of emotions: apprehension, excitement, curiosity, and for some, a ho-hum-I'd-rather-be-playing-outside look. But one student in the third row sent a signal that stood out from the rest. Charonne wondered about the story behind the child's apparent fear, and she asked God to show her how to help that little girl feel safe.

Jennifer was a beautiful girl with long blond hair and big blue eyes. On rare occasions she would crack a smile that would melt any heart. During recess, Jennifer typically pulled away by herself while the rest of the class played in groups. When the other girls tried to include her, she refused to acknowledge their acts of friendship. She swatted away Charonne's efforts to reach out to her as if they were pesky mosquitoes on a hot summer night. Phone calls to her parents were never returned. Penetrating the rock walls around Jennifer's heart seemed like an impossible assignment.

Lord, why is this little girl so sad? What am I to do to help her? Charonne prayed.

The only answer that came was, *She needs your love.*

Jennifer's parents did not come to the parent-teacher conferences in October. In November, the school held an open house. The children designed personalized folders and collected special papers they wanted to show their parents. Knowing no one would show up, Jennifer took her folder home. That's how it was all year long. Charonne even tried contacting the aunt who had enrolled Jennifer in the school, but she hit one dead end after another.

Lord, I know that You put Jennifer in my class for a reason. I know that You want me to love her, but I feel so inadequate. I don't know how to break through the walls. I don't know how to love her the way she needs to be loved.

It was a tough first assignment for a young teacher fresh out of college. Charonne had been hired to teach reading, writing, and arithmetic; college hadn't taught her how to solve complex problems like this one. There were nights she cried herself to sleep over the obvious pain she read in this little girl's eyes. But she consistently prayed for the children and tried her best to love them day in and day out.

Then, shortly before Thanksgiving, something curious happened. Charonne was reading a story to the class. The students were gathered around her, and Jennifer was seated directly at her feet. In the middle of the story Jennifer quietly stood, moved the book Charonne was reading aside, and crawled onto Charonne's lap. After laying her head on Charonne's chest, she moved the book back into place and put her thumb in her mouth, acknowledging that it was okay for Charonne to continue. Charonne gently wrapped her arm around the needy little girl, trying hard to swallow the big lump that had suddenly appeared in her throat.

The pages of the book blurred through Charonne's tears, but somehow she was able to collect herself and finish the story. This happened many times throughout the year. The other children in class seemed to be graced with a special understanding of Jennifer's needs. Not one of them ever said a word or made an issue of her story-time behavior.

A bitterly cold winter arrived early that year, and by early December there was a blanket of snow on the ground. Jennifer came to school wearing only a thin sweater to shield her from the harsh elements.

"Do you have a coat to wear?" Charonne asked.

"No," came the quick reply, "but it doesn't matter. I never get cold."

After several unsuccessful attempts to reach Jennifer's parents, Charonne brought a coat to school to give Jennifer. Jennifer and the coat became inseparable. Rather than hanging it on the wall with the other children's jackets, she clung to that coat as if it were the only one she would ever have the rest of her life. It never left her presence. Whenever she was in the classroom, she laid it carefully across her lap or tucked it securely under her arm.

Christmas vacation arrived, and the children in the class bubbled with delight as they discussed the gifts they wanted Santa to bring them. Jennifer said nothing. As the students bundled up to leave for their two-week break, Jennifer broke the silence. "Teacher, I don't want to go."

Her initiation caught Charonne by surprise. She asked Jennifer if her mother was coming to get her.

"No, my dad is coming because he just lost his job," she replied. She asked to sit on Charonne's lap.

Charonne helped Jennifer zip her coat, gave her a hug, and then pulled her up onto her lap. They sat in silence for a time, Jennifer's arms wrapped tightly around Charonne's neck. Then the little girl jumped down and headed out the door of the room. Charonne tried to walk her down the hall, but Jennifer said, "No! Please stay here!"

Charonne honored Jennifer's request and went to the window to wave good-bye. It was difficult to watch the sweet little girl wiping tears from her cheeks as she got into her father's car.

After the holidays, Jennifer didn't return to class. The principal said that the family had moved out of district. Charonne's heart ached. She had not prayed for Jennifer during all the busy events of the holidays. Story time was difficult. The whole class seemed to feel that something was missing. In a few short months, the little girl in the third row had left her mark on their hearts, and they missed her.

Then late in January, without any prior notification, Jennifer reappeared in class. She said nothing about where she had been or why she had been gone. When asked about her absence, she made it clear that she didn't want to talk about it. The children respected her wishes and seemed to pick up right where they had left off.

Toward the end of April, Charonne was given her teaching assignment for the following year: a combined class of first and second graders. Once again Jennifer was on her list. Charonne leaped at the chance to have another year to help this emotionally fragile little girl.

Jennifer was a bright child and learned quickly. Math and reading came easy for her, and she tried desperately to please Charonne in all she did. She was always the first one in class to complete her work and frequently asked if there was anything she could do to help Charonne. After school each day, Jennifer typically lingered in the classroom, as her ride often arrived very late. Charonne took advantage of the time to visit with Jennifer, affirm her worth, and plant seeds of hope in her soul.

On the last day of school before summer vacation, Charonne stood at the door, giving out words of encouragement and hugs as she bade the children good-bye. After all the other students had left, Jennifer, once again, approached Charonne and asked to sit on her lap. Much to Charonne's surprise this precious little girl wrapped her arms around her neck and began to sob uncontrollably.

After a very long wait, Jennifer's mother finally came to the classroom to get her. When Charonne stood to greet Mrs. Warner, she did not respond. Turning her attention to Jennifer, she snapped sharply, *"Come now,* Jenny!"

Jennifer dropped her teacher's hand, picked up her things, and then gave Charonne one more hug before silently leaving the room. Charonne stood, frozen in her tracks, unable to absorb what had just happened. Then, in a last-ditch effort to build a bridge with the family, she called out once again to Mrs. Warner. But the mother spun quickly around and angrily barked, "You handle her at school, and I will handle her at home," and stomped down the hallway in a huff. The words stung. Noticing the embarrassment on Jennifer's face, Charonne smiled and nodded at the little girl as if to say, "It's okay, honey—I understand."

During the summer break, Jennifer called Charonne at home a couple of times. The visits were brief, and both times Jennifer mentioned how she could hardly wait until school started again in the fall.

As the new school year got underway, Charonne marveled at the growth and development she witnessed in her returning students. Summer had been good to them all. Everyone, that is, except Jennifer. She seemed more remote and regressive in her interactions with the children, satisfied to observe rather than to participate.

The fall season passed quickly. One afternoon, at the end of a school day shortly before Christmas vacation, the children scurried to get their coats and catch their rides. Jennifer hugged Charonne good-bye and then raced down the hallway and out the door.

When Charonne walked back to her desk there was a tattered, dirty envelope that said, "To my teacher to keep forever." Charonne carefully broke the seal. Inside was a small picture of Jennifer. Charonne did not realize at the time that Jennifer would never return to her classroom. Again, she and her family suddenly disappeared, with no explanation to anyone at school.

Many years came and went. And then one afternoon the phone rang, and Jennifer was on the other end of the line. She had called to see how Charonne was and asked to hear all about her students and her family. Charonne told her about the births of her two sons. They visited for a few minutes and then Jennifer suddenly interrupted the conversation. "I love you. Good-bye," she said. A cloud of sadness descended over Charonne. Once again this precious girl had entered her life and then abruptly exited without warning.

Over the years Charonne prayed for Jennifer and kept her picture in her wallet along with other prized family photos. On one occasion, Charonne misplaced her purse. After looking for it in every conceivable place, she gave up hope and prayed that God would somehow return her wallet to her.

More than a year had passed when a large envelope with no return address was delivered to Charonne's house. Inside, Charonne found her wallet intact, with all of her pictures in place, including Jennifer's. Taking Jennifer's picture from the old wallet, she placed it in her new one and once again prayed for the little girl who had once sat in the third row.

Nineteen years later, Charonne was invited to speak at a conference for women. While collecting her teaching materials at the end of a session, a beautiful young lady approached her. "Do you remember me?" she asked, reaching to shake Charonne's hand.

As Charonne searched the unfamiliar face for a clue, the woman's eyes solved the mystery. There before her were those same beautiful blue eyes that had looked at her from the third row in her classroom. "Yes!" Charonne exclaimed with joy. "I know who you are—you are Jennifer!"

As they hugged and cried, the story of a broken little girl unfolded. Jennifer's mother had died when Jennifer was fourteen, leaving her and her younger brother in the hands of a cruel stepfather. Jennifer thought many times of running away from his brutal rage and sexual abuse, but she feared for her little brother's life. She had stayed for his sake.

Charonne gathered Jennifer into her arms and listened carefully.

"I gave my heart to Jesus one summer during a vacation Bible school. Through all the bad stuff that happened, I always knew that there was someone who loved me and that that someone was my teacher. But when your arms were not there for me, God held me. When I couldn't find your lap, I climbed up onto His."

Jennifer paused, wiped her eyes, swallowed hard, and asked: "Did you keep it forever?"

Memories of that tattered, dirty envelope, lying on her desk nearly twenty years before, flooded in. Charonne reached into her purse, pulled out her wallet, opened it to Jennifer's picture and smiled, "Yes, Jennifer. I kept it forever."

Power Perks: A Sip of Hope and Humor

God carries your picture in His wallet.

Tony Campolo

I can look back at my darkest periods and realize that these were the times when the Lord was holding me closest. But I couldn't see his face because my face was in his breast crying.

John Michael Talbot

God loves each of us as if there were only one of us.

Saint Augustine of Hippo

Lord, you know the hopes of humble people. Surely you will hear their cries and comfort their hearts by helping them.

Psalm 10:17, TLB

Power Perks: A Sip of Hope and Humor

The only way God's love makes sense is when it is seen as personal (not mechanical). He doesn't start your car for you; but he comes and sits with you in the snowbank.

Robert F. Capon

God works powerfully, but for the most part gently and gradually.

John Newton

My response is to get down on my knees before the Father, this magnificent Father who parcels out all heaven and earth. I ask him to strengthen you by his Spirit—not a brute strength but a glorious inner strength—that Christ will live in you as you open the door and invite him in. And I ask him that with both feet planted firmly on love, you'll be able to take in with all Christians the extravagant dimensions of Christ's love. Reach out and experience the breadth! Test its length! Plumb the depths! Rise to the heights! Live full lives, full in the fullness of God.

God can do anything, you know—far more than you could ever imagine or guess or request in your wildest dreams! He does it not by pushing us around but by working within us, his Spirit deeply and gently within us.

Ephesians 3:14–20, *The Message*

CHAPTER 16

A Dream Come True

*J*esus said, *"Ask and it will be given to you."*

Matthew 7:7

I suppose that every young girl dreams about being swept off her feet by a knight in shining armor. But we all define the shining armor differently. Some girls wish for a handsome, hunky guy. Others long for a musical genius, a wealthy Wall Street wizard, or the thoughtful, poetic type.

My aunt, Charlene Walker, prayed for something altogether different. Her story is a reminder that the Lord hears the simple prayers of a little child. As you'll see, He answered in a rather creative way.

Let her story encourage you: Your dreams matter to God. Never underestimate His ability to weave a beautiful plan in your life.

When I was a young girl, I learned that I had the rarest type of blood, AB/RH-negative. An extremely small percentage of the population falls into this category. In those days this posed a serious problem for women during childbearing years because antibodies that naturally form in RH-negative blood can harm babies in utero. No medications were available to inhibit this process. With each new pregnancy, antibodies increase in the bloodstream, creating a risk to the life of the baby. My doctor told me that unless I married a man with RH-negative blood, I would likely be unable to have more than one child.

This was distressing news to me because I was an only child, and I had hoped to have a large family. When he was two years old, my brother had accidentally drowned, and my mother had lost four other babies because of RH-negative complications. I left the doctor's office that day very troubled, but I turned my fear to prayer: I asked God to please give me an RH-negative husband when I grew up.

Many years passed. I graduated from nursing school and was working in a hospital when I received a letter from a young man overseas named Jim. I had never met him, but his army buddy was a college chum of mine. He had seen my picture in his buddy's wallet and wondered if I was "a loyal American citizen who would write to a lonely soldier in Korea."

For two years I sent Jim cards on special occasions, and we exchanged letters and pictures. Eventually the army rotated him back to the States and assigned him to duty as a range officer. He was up by five o'clock every morning to set up the range. During his downtime before the troops arrived, he faithfully wrote me a heartfelt letter a day. We became well acquainted through the mail and eventually decided that we should meet in person.

Jim took leave during the Christmas holidays in 1955. I still remember his first words. With an effervescent smile and an expansive embrace he said, "You're even prettier than your pictures!" Three days later he asked me to marry him. I don't think he expected to hear the words that came out of my mouth.

"Jim," I blurted out, "I can only marry a man with RH-negative blood!"

Rocking with laughter, he responded, "You've got him, baby!"

Postscript: Jim and Charlene were married on June 29, 1956, and today have four children and sixteen grandchildren. They pray daily for each generation and also for their grandchildren's future partners in life.

Power Perks: A Sip of Hope and Humor

In a perfect world, men would not be allowed to drive because of territorial tendencies and women would not be allowed access to the remote control. The instinct to "nest" is just way too strong.

Dan Chriestenson

A couple that had been married for twenty-five years celebrated their sixtieth birthdays. During the party a fairy appeared and said that because they had been such a loving couple all those years, she would give them one wish each.

The wife wanted to travel around the world. The fairy waved her wand and *boom!* She had the tickets in her hand.

Next, it was the husband's turn. He paused for a moment, and then said shyly, "Well, I'd like to be married to a woman thirty years younger than I am."

The fairy picked up her wand and *boom!* He was ninety!

Every time I close the door on reality it comes in through the windows.

Jennifer Unlimited

One of my clients was at her wits' end over being pestered by her boss. While driving down the freeway she prayed, *Oh, God, what am I going to do?* No sooner had those words escaped her mouth than a pest control van passed her with a huge sign on the back that read, HELP IS ON THE WAY! Who says God doesn't have a sense of humor?

The same Lord is Lord of all and richly blesses all who call on him.

Romans 10:12

CHAPTER 17

Can I fill That Cup for You?

*H*e satisfies the thirsty and fills the hungry with good things.
Psalm 107:9

"Yes, I'll do the interview," I told the media company while I jotted *Radio Show—5:30 A.M.* on my September calendar. A station on the East Coast wanted to do a live talk show featuring my book *Empty Arms,* which I wrote to comfort and support those in the deep grief following a baby's death through stillbirth, miscarriage, or tubal pregnancy.

The evening before the broadcast, I set the timer on the coffeepot and my alarm for 5:00 A.M. so I would be wide awake, coffee'd up, and ready to roll for the interview. It was still dark outside when the show's host called to talk with me about the disappointment and heartache of losing a baby. When she asked me to talk about the death of our baby, the memories were vividly fresh, though seventeen years had passed since our loss.

"Does time really heal all wounds?" she asked. "Can you think about your baby without mourning?"

"Healing comes in bits and pieces, over a period of time," I commented. "Researchers used to say the grieving process typically lasted between eighteen and twenty-four months. Now the projections are much greater—as high as five years or more, depending on the type of loss we've suffered."

I reflected on my own experience: "Every year, for seven years, when February 4 arrived, I grieved. That was the day I went to the hospital, delivered our baby, and went home with empty arms. It wasn't until eight years after our loss that I realized that February 4 had come and gone and the painful memories hadn't surfaced. I'm seventeen years out from that loss today, and while I can clearly remember the events, much of the pain has lost its power."

We went on to talk about the emotional and spiritual confusion that parents feel when a baby dies, and I tried to offer words of support and comfort to those in the listening audience. The interview ended, and I moved on to the other responsibilities of the day.

Jump ahead three weeks. It was the end of a very long day, and I was in a funk. John had flown out of town that morning with three friends to fish in Alaska. I saw him out the door, sent the kids off to school, and went to the counseling center for a full day of meeting with clients.

Two appointments into the day, I received a call from Nathan's school. Just hearing "The school is on the line for you" ties my stomach in knots because of some of his previous shenanigans at school. (You can read the lively, hair-raising details of those stories in the first two Espresso books.)

"It's the school nurse," my assistant, Betty, told me.

I picked up the phone. "Hello, this is Pam," I said, holding my breath.

"It appears that Nathan has a rash on the back of his neck," the nurse said. "Has he had the chicken pox?"

I assured her that he had and that the rash might have been due to his not rinsing the shampoo out of his hair well enough the night before. He had wanted to wash his hair by himself, so we let him. *Oops.*

"We need you to come and get him because we don't know what this rash is or if it's contagious."

My schedule was booked solid with back-to-back clients. John was out of town. Now this. "I'll have to make some calls and get back to you. I'm not sure how I'm going to work this out," I told her. I called several friends who typically would pinch-hit for me in an emergency like this. One friend was at the hospital with her daughter, who was in the middle of a serious procedure. Another was taking her sick dog to the vet. Two others didn't answer their phones.

I called the school back to let the nurse know that I was working on making arrangements, but she told me that I needed to come for Nathan *now*. The nurses' station was overloaded with children, and the health rules would not allow Nathan to return to class with a rash.

I had no alternative but to cancel my appointments, pick up Nathan, and take him to the doctor. Come to find out, it was simple, noncontagious dermatitis. By the time we left the doctor's office, I had "my knickers in a twist," as my great-grandmother used to put it. It was her nice way of saying that I had a bad attitude. And, like Nathan's rash, it was spreading quickly!

The irritations didn't stop there. Driving my son Ben to his football practice, some guy in a beat-up old jalopy kept tailgating me. I tapped my brakes, hoping he would pick up the signal to get off my bumper. He didn't. Instead, he whipped out from behind me into the right lane and floored it. Much to his dismay, another car was just ahead, and it effectively blocked him from passing. So what did he do? He braked, whipped his car back behind me, and settled back on my bumper. Something told me that *his* knickers were askew as well.

We were driving north, approaching a major intersection, when a police car, traveling west, was proceeding through a red light with his lights flashing and siren blaring. The driver in front of me suddenly slammed on his brakes, and I in turn stomped on mine to avoid a collision.

But the guy behind me was way too close. Yup, you guessed it: Before I could blink, the back end of my car was history.

Suffice it to say, it was not a good day. I tucked the kids in that night, crawled in my bed, and covered my head, not wanting anything more to do with anyone. I figured the next day had to be better.

Morning dawned, the kids left for school, and I plopped down at my desk to write a chapter for this book. I worked on bits and pieces I had started the week before, but it was one of those days when my mind was as slow as molasses on a January morning and my fingers were equally clumsy. One idea flowed into another about as smoothly as my two-car collision the day before. After a few hours, I finally shut off my computer, wondering if my investment in it had even been worth it.

Breathing a discouraged sigh, I decided to check the mail. There, amid the stack of envelopes in the box, was a letter from a woman on the East Coast. She had heard the radio talk show a few weeks earlier. Come to find out, she had read *Empty Arms* fifteen years ago following the loss of her second baby. But the book had been more than a grief manual for her—it had been a stepping stone to a relationship with God! "After reading *Empty Arms,* I invited God to become a part of my life, and He helped me heal," she wrote. "I don't usually write authors, but something kept pressing me to send you a note." Once again I marveled at the magnitude of God's love and grace. He knew I had the blues that day and that I needed encouragement. And He used a woman…

- who lived clear across the country,
- whom I had never met,
- who had happened to read one of my books *fifteen years* ago,
- who had stumbled upon the radio broadcast three weeks before,
- who knew nothing of my present predicament,
- who had just the words to speak to my need and remind me that my writing mattered.

Indeed, God is good.

I hear enough stories in the counseling office to know that I'm not the only one who has sat on the edge of a bed in the morning and asked, *Is it worth it all?* Second-guessing life is a malady common to all of us, particularly when we're tired and our energy reserves have been sapped by one stress after another.

That's the plight of a thirsty soul. When life shoots holes in the bottom of our cup, draining us dry, we feel as if there aren't enough of us to go around, and we wonder if we're doing anybody any good. Maxwell House coffee may be good to the last drop, but I know I'm not. The last few drops in the bottom of my personal cup are usually full of discouragement and pessimism. I find some comfort in knowing that I'm not alone.

Isn't it amazing that just a few words, jotted down quickly and mailed, can transform someone's hopeless day into an energized one? That the simple act of putting pen to paper can revive a weary spirit? That flowery words mean less than earnest ones when it comes to caring? That's the power of one little note of encouragement—one perfectly timed, divinely inspired word of thanks from an unexpected source. It brings us back to our senses, reminding us of what investments matter most—loving God and others in whatever way we can.

Are you up for a challenge? Why not fill someone's cup today with a word of blessing? Ask the Lord to give you the name of one friend who needs to be reminded that he or she is loved and appreciated.

Lisa's name just came to my mind. So if you'll excuse me, I'll end the story here. It's time for me to find some stationery!

Power Perks: A Sip of Hope and Humor

The small change of human happiness lies in the unexpected friendly word.

Elizabeth Harrison

Be steadfast, immovable, always abounding in the work of the Lord, knowing that your toil is not in vain in the Lord.

1 Corinthians 15:58, NASB

A good word costs no more than a bad one.

English proverb

He climbs highest who helps another.

Zig Ziglar

More people fail for lack of encouragement than for any other reason.

Let's keep a firm grip on the promises that keep us going. He always keeps his word. Let's see how inventive we can be in encouraging love and helping out.

Hebrews 10:23–24, *The Message*

A man was in a supermarket pushing a cart that contained a screaming, bellowing baby. The gentleman kept repeating softly, "Don't get excited, Albert. Don't scream, Albert. Don't yell, Albert. Keep calm, Albert."

A woman standing next to him said, "You certainly are to be commended for trying to soothe your son."

The man looked at her. "Lady, *I'm* Albert."

CHAPTER 18

Garage Sale Treasures

*S*tore up for yourselves treasures in heaven, where neither moth nor rust destroys, and where thieves do not break in or steal; for where your treasure is, there your heart will be also.

Matthew 6:20–21, NASB

If it's Friday morning, you'll find Kelly hunting for garage and estate sales. She is forever in search of unexpected riches that someone wants to get rid of for a buck or two. She has found some amazing treasures over the years, but none as valuable as what she discovered at Jennifer's garage sale.

A woman was manning two tables in the parking lot of her low-income housing apartment. When Kelly arrived, a full assortment of household knickknacks and doodads were on display.

Hmmmm, Kelly thought. *What little gem can I find here?* Browsing the tables, she picked up three miniature woodcarvings that were crafted with the finest attention to detail. "How much for these?" she asked, not raising her head to see who was standing behind the table.

"I'll have to ask my friend," came the reply. "They belong to his mother." Kelly looked up to find a tiny, tired-looking woman with stringy, long brown hair. As Kelly continued to peruse the tables and pick up items of interest, the frail woman took another drag of her cigarette, blew the smoke off to the left, and began to tell Kelly some stories. A little about this. A little about that. But mostly about herself. "I'm losing my government housing because I refused to pay the rent until they fixed the leak in my ceiling. They don't care about the leak, so out we go. Thought I'd make a few dollars before they lock me out."

Kelly is a kind, compassionate soul, and the woman's story stopped her in her tracks. She paused, turned toward the woman, set down the items she was holding, and gave her her undivided attention.

Pleased, the woman continued. Kelly learned that the woman had two sons with cerebral palsy. Tony was fourteen, and Chris was ten. They were the joys of her life. She had left the boys' father a while back to save her life and theirs. Apparently he abused them to maintain control. Convinced that nothing would be as bad as living with that man, the woman packed up her boys and headed for the streets, leaving everything behind.

Kelly was moved. Now that they were conversing, she

thought that she should introduce herself. "My name is Kelly," she said. "It's so nice to meet you." She extended her hand across the table.

With a firm grasp the woman shook her hand and responded, "Thanks, I'm Jennifer. Hey, look! Here comes Tony."

A young man walked across the parking lot with an uncertain gait and a huge smile on his face that would melt your heart. Jennifer introduced her son to Kelly, who greeted him warmly. Then Kelly prepared to leave. "I'll come back tomorrow and check on those figurines, okay?" she said.

Jennifer nodded and said that she'd ask about the prices.

But when Kelly drove home that day, she knew she was going to return for more than three wooden carvings. God was tugging on her heart to reach out to three hurting people who desperately needed His love.

That evening Kelly sat with her husband, Aaron, on the family-room couch watching their children play. Jennifer's plight weighed heavily on Kelly's mind. *How can she hold up under the burden of not knowing where she and her children will go next?* she mused silently.

That's about the time Kelly's practical side kicked into gear. She told Aaron about her newfound friends, and together they brainstormed some ways to help. They decided that, if nothing else, they could feed Jennifer and the boys at their pizza parlor. Wallstreet Pizza has been a household name in the Portland area for many years. Everyone knows that Wallstreet has some of the best New York–style pizza in town. Aaron and Kelly could at least make sure that Jennifer and her children would not go hungry. They could have all the pizza, salad, sandwiches, garlic rolls, and drinks their stomachs could hold.

The next morning, Kelly went back to Jennifer's parking lot, purchased the three delicate wooden carvings, and then invited Jennifer and the boys to Wallstreet for "dinner on the house" that evening. The boys lit up, displaying an obvious enthusiasm for pizza, pop, and pinball fun. The conversation continued.

"Do you have a church?" Kelly asked, thinking that some spiritual support and fellowship might be helpful during their time of transition.

"I've gone to a few services at a church down the road," Jennifer replied, "but I kinda feel like I don't fit in. There's another church I've wanted to try, but I'm too scared to go alone. Will you go with me?"

"I sure will!" Kelly responded, excitement in her voice.

The next day the two women slipped into the back row of the church. Jennifer had come alone, wanting to make sure the church would be a good fit before bringing the boys along. As soon as the music started, Jennifer began wiping tears from her eyes. Kelly reached over and patted her gently on the shoulder.

"I'm so sorry," Jennifer apologized. "It's just that I've

been fighting this battle alone for so long."

"It's okay," Kelly assured her. "Everything is going to be all right."

Kelly and Aaron felt that the Lord wanted them to help this family in more tangible ways. They rented a hotel room for several weeks for Jennifer and the boys so the family would have a place to stay until they could make more permanent arrangements.

But embracing an unfamiliar kind of love can be difficult. A few months into their friendship, Jennifer bolted. She didn't feel worthy of Kelly and Aaron's love. The shame was too overwhelming. Not wanting to be a financial burden to anyone, Jennifer disappeared with her sons. Kelly and Aaron later found out that she and the boys had settled into a flooded, dark, creepy basement apartment. After a near-fatal spider bite sent Jennifer to the hospital, she reluctantly contacted Aaron and Kelly. Once again, this generous couple stepped in to help.

Aaron and Kelly rented a small, older house on a little lot right behind the church that Jennifer wanted to attend. A group of ladies from Kelly's Bible study furnished each room from stem to stern. They made a fun day of it, stocking the cupboards with pretty plates, bowls, and glasses, the drawers with silverware and cooking utensils, and the refrigerator with food enough to feed an army. Jennifer wouldn't have to shop for weeks. They decked out the bathroom with fluffy, clean towels, soaps, lotions, and all the necessities a woman and two young men would need.

It was the week before Christmas. You need to know this about Kelly: If you were to visit her house at Christmastime, you would walk into a winter wonderland. Kelly is a first-class decorator with a real knack for taking something simple and turning it into something spectacular. So it didn't surprise me that she and the ladies decorated for Christmas at Jennifer's place too. Twinkly bright lights glittered from the mantel, and Christmas music filled the rooms when Jennifer and her boys walked through the front door of their new home.

Glancing around the room, her eyes as big as saucers, Jennifer could hardly take it all in. Collapsing on the couch and sobbing aloud, she cried, "I've never known love like this. Never!"

When Kelly told me this story, tears rose in my eyes. I didn't even know Jennifer, but I wanted to hug her. Swallowing the golf ball in my throat, I asked, "Kelly, how has this changed your life?" Her words still ring in my ears.

"The truth is," Kelly said, "I needed Jennifer more than she needed me. She has taught me about the heart of God. When I look at her raising her handicapped sons, suffering with Hepatitis C and uterine cancer, I feel His heart beat for her. He has placed His compassion in my heart for her. I'm just a vessel to deliver His love.

"And during the last year and a half that I've known Jennifer, God has made me face some things about myself,"

Kelly admitted. "He has redefined for me the true meaning of joy. Every time I hold Jennifer in my arms, the joy is so great that I feel like my heart is going to burst. That kind of joy doesn't come from owning a big house, running a successful business, or from any of the stuff money can buy. It comes as a reward from God for being used by Him to fulfill His purposes. As I laid down my treasures, I received His. Since I've known Jennifer I've had to grapple with some important questions. I have sensed God asking me:

> Can I entrust My broken ones to you?
> Will you cry out for their transformation?
> Will you trade in your priestly robe for a cloak of humility?
> Will you lay down your life for those in need?
> Will you stand by them and hold their hands as I change them?
> Will you extend your hand in love?

"'If you do,' He seemed to say, 'I will come alongside you and place My hand upon yours. The power of My love will strengthen you and together we will pull them out of the mire.'"

Jesus commands us to "love one another" so that our joy will be full.

Kelly went hunting for treasures at a parking lot garage sale. Jennifer and her boys were the priceless treasures she found.

What treasures live near you?

Power Perks: A Sip of Hope and Humor

What God sends is better than what man asks for.

After the friendship of God, a friend's affection is the greatest treasure here below.

Treasures in heaven are laid up as treasures on earth are laid down.

The photographer for a national magazine was assigned to shoot a great forest fire. He was told that a small plane would be waiting to take him over the fire.

He arrived at the airstrip just an hour before sundown. Sure enough, the Cessna was waiting. He jumped in with his equipment and shouted, "Let's go!" The pilot swung the plane into the wind and soon they were in the air.

"Fly over the north side of the fire," said the photographer, "and make several low-level passes."

"Why?" asked the nervous pilot.

"Because I'm going to take pictures!" retorted the photographer. "I'm a photographer, and photographers take pictures."

After a long pause, the pilot asked, "You mean, you're not the instructor?"

Steve Farrar[1]

Some wish to live within the sound of church and chapel bell. I wish to run a rescue mission within a yard of hell.

Charles Thomas Studd

Money is a good servant, but a dangerous master.

Dominique Bouhours

CHAPTER 19

Adolescent Escapades

The deeds of a man's hands will return to him.

Proverbs 12:14, NASB

As a boy growing up in the rural culture of Northwestern Montana in the early seventies, Steve Huggins learned that there were certain skills no self-respecting adolescent male should lack. These included horseback riding, roping, and marksmanship. The riding and roping he acquired as a matter of course while hanging out with friends on the ranch. Marksmanship, however, required more work.

Steve and his brother wandered the local landscape hour after hour, blasting thousands of rounds of BBs into most anything that would improve their proficiency. They successfully killed thousands of sticks, rocks, mud puddles, pop cans, and a few unfortunate birds and rodents that let them get too close. In time, Steve was able to hit a penny from a fair distance, sending it ricocheting this direction and that.

One sunny, hot day, good fortune came Steve's way. His parents told him that they were going on a picnic with family friends near their favorite fishing hole and gave him permission to bring his BB gun. He knew the path to the stream well. It wound through acres and acres where he could shoot his gun. What a day! The skies were blue, Mom was bringing her famous apple pie, and life was about as good as it could get for a twelve-year-old boy in Montana.

After their lip-smacking lunch, the dads meandered down toward the water to fish while Steve sat at the wooden picnic table beside the rippling creek reloading his gun with a few hundred BBs. He was distracted when his mother and her friend, who also happened to be his piano and Sunday school teacher, stood up and walked away. Watching them stroll through the grass raised some scientific questions that Steve couldn't seem to shake from his mind: *Just how far can a BB travel? And how fast does one move?*

Questions screamed for answers. As the ladies walked away, Steve rested his BB gun across the picnic table and carefully sighted in on the posterior of his Sunday school teacher. No evil motives were involved—he was simply conducting an experiment in the name of science. Ever so slowly, he squeezed the trigger.

Wham!

That shiny brass BB shot out of the end of the rifle, traveling farther and straighter than any BB he had ever shot before. It didn't veer even one centimeter off its entire twenty-five-foot course. Then *smack*—it hit the target dead center. (I told you he was working on his proficiency.)

Steve almost swallowed his tongue when he realized what he had done. *I'm doomed! My life is over! Death is near!* he thought. Panicked, he buried his face in his hands.

The next thing Steve heard was "Whooopppeeee!" Peering through his fingers, he saw his teacher swatting her backside with her hand. She and Steve's mother whirled in his direction with blazing eyes and pursed lips that said, "Buddy—you're dead meat!"

Although his teacher was a bit sore, Steve says that the only thing that was really hurt was his ego. It's hard to maintain a macho image when you have to tell the other guys in town that you can't carry a gun because "Mom and Dad took it away." Steve's parents signed him up for hunter safety classes, and his career as "scientist" was short-lived.

Steve went on to become an outstanding all-American marine, a clinical psychologist, a devoted husband, and the father of two girls. With one of his daughters now approaching her thirteenth birthday, Steve plans to get some mileage out of his adolescent escapade. The next time they swap stories around the family table, he plans to drive home the morals of the story: *If you aim at nothing, you're sure to hit it. So set goals. Think carefully about what you shoot for in life—you're likely to hit it. And consider the consequences before taking aim— once things are set in motion, there may be a point of no return.*

Why Parents Get Gray Hair

The boss of a big company needed to call one of his employees about an urgent problem with one of the main computers. He dialed the employee's home phone number and was greeted with a child's whispered, "Hello?"

Feeling put out at the inconvenience of having to talk to a youngster, the boss asked, "Is your daddy home?"

"Yes," whispered the small voice.

"May I talk with him?" the man asked.

To his surprise, the small voice whispered, "No, he's very busy."

Wanting to talk with an adult, the boss asked, "Is your mommy there?"

"Yes," came the answer.

"May I talk with her?"

Again the small voice whispered, "No, she's very busy."

The boss decided that he would just leave a message. "Is anyone there besides you?" the boss asked the child.

"Yes" whispered the child. "A policeman."

Wondering what a cop would be doing at his employee's home, the boss asked, "May I speak with the policeman?"

"No, he's very busy," whispered the child.

"Busy doing what?" asked the boss.

"Talking to Daddy and Mommy and the fireman."

The boss heard what sounded like a helicopter through the phone. Growing concerned, he asked, "What is that noise?"

"A hello-copper," answered the child.

Now alarmed, the boss asked, "What is going on there?"

Power Perks: A Sip of Hope and Humor

"O-o-h-h…" the child whispered in awe, "the search team just landed the hello-copter."

More than just a little frustrated, the boss asked, "Why are they there?"

Still whispering, the young voice replied in a muffled giggle: "They're looking for me."

Sow a thought and you reap an act;
    Sow an act and you reap a habit;
Sow a habit and you reap a character;
    Sow a character and you reap a destiny.

Samuel Smiles

CHAPTER 20

God Hears Your Silence, and He Speaks

esus said,] "My sheep listen to my voice, and I know them, and they follow me."

John 10:27

I phoned her one afternoon. Like me, she is a mother with a handicapped son. She had written me a letter after reading *Angel Behind the Rocking Chair: Stories of Hope in Unexpected Places.* I was so moved by her letter that I just had to talk with her. Though she lives on the East Coast and I live on the West Coast, it was as if the space between us didn't exist. There was an instant connection when we spoke of what we had in common.

But I'm getting ahead of myself. Let me step aside for a moment so you can hear Ginny declare firsthand the unfailing grace of God. In the letter she sent, she wrote:

I, too, have a son who is handicapped. Tommy has been quadriplegic for the last nineteen years. He is now thirty-three and cannot move other than to shrug his shoulders and move his head. These last nineteen years I have struggled with my faith, trying to understand how a young boy of fourteen could have his life so horribly ripped away from him. There are times when I cannot even pray because the sorrow is so deep. During those times, I ask God to look into my heart and hear my silence. I believe that He does.

Your book, *Angel Behind the Rocking Chair*, consoled me and opened my eyes to see that God is in control, that we are where we are supposed to be in life, and that, if God wants us somewhere else, He will orchestrate things to get us there. You, too, understand the loss of dreams, both for my husband, Tom, and me, and our son, Tommy. I have two other children who have had less time from their mother and father due to Tommy's special needs. Beth was seven, and Danny was eleven when Tommy was injured. However, they have grown up and become beautiful, caring, responsible adults, and we are very proud of them.

I wanted to tell you about a time in our life when we knew without a doubt that God had spoken to us. It happened after Tommy's accident, when he was fighting for his life with the help of a respirator. The doctor told us that Tommy would never breathe again on his own. His injury was too high on his neck, all the way up to the C-3 disc. My husband repeatedly argued with the physician, insisting that Tommy would breathe again without the machines. On one occasion the doctor was so furious with my husband that he yelled, "What the 'blankety-blank' is wrong with you? Why can't you accept the fact that your son will never again breathe on his own?"

My husband simply said, *"No!* We are all praying for a miracle."

It seemed as if our every waking breath was a prayer. Night and day we stayed by Tommy's side, hoping things would take a turn for the better.

Our wedding anniversary, May 29, was shortly after Tommy's injury. Some friends gave us fifty dollars with a stern admonition to get away from the hospital and go out to dinner. Following their advice, we made reservations at a nice restaurant and tried our best to be grateful for the break. We enjoyed a lovely meal together in warm, peaceful surroundings. It was a welcome reprieve from the cold, sterile hospital room with blipping screens surrounding Tommy.

When we got home, Tom poured a couple of

glasses of champagne, and we toasted one another and reminisced about all we had been through together. Then, in the middle of our conversation, things took an odd twist. Out of the blue, Tom glanced up from his glass of champagne and said, "God just spoke to me. He told me that Tommy's breathing will improve tomorrow and that he will be able to come off the respirator." I didn't say much, figuring his ideas were a combination of wishful thinking and champagne.

The next morning we drove back to the hospital. As we were getting off the elevator on Tommy's floor, an excited nurse came charging at us waving her hands wildly to grab our attention.

"Did you hear what Tommy did this morning? Did you hear? He registered high enough on the monitor that we can start weaning him off the respirator!"

I froze in stunned silence; my husband's smile lit up the entire ward. God had clearly spoken to him. He knew it. I knew it. And eventually, the doctors and nurses knew it too.

During the last nineteen years, we have witnessed many more miracles. I am certain that in each of these circumstances God was speaking, guiding, and comforting us, particularly through the first few horrible years after Tommy's injury.

Someday I will document those miracles. There are many.

Tommy still cannot walk, move his arms and hands, or feed himself. But he is with us, and he is a very important part of our family. He is a strong, courageous, compassionate man void of self-pity. He brings us great joy, and he is a wonderful big brother despite his handicaps.

Has life been hard? God knows—*yes!* Every day presents a new set of challenges and grievous reminders of what could have been had it not been for the accident. But through it all, God has been with us, carrying us along, one day at a time. Tommy graduated from high school and earned an associate degree in computer programming. A while back he started a small business as a computer programmer. Last year he was invited to deliver the keynote address to the graduating class at the college he attended many years ago. He was awarded Alumni of the Year. I could go on and on, but I'll stop now. I just wanted to thank you, Pam, for leading me out of the desert with your book.

After reading Ginny's closing remarks, I folded up the letter, wiped the tears off my cheeks and chin, and stared into the crackling fire in front of me. I understood her heartache. All I could think was, *Where would any of us be without You, Lord?*

The answer for me was obvious. I'd have given up long ago. Ginny's story drove home a truth I have come to understand more fully in the last eight years: There is no problem big enough to exhaust God's help. There is no form of suffering big enough to tax His abilities. There is no difficulty God cannot handle. And there is no painful situation we cannot endure if we look to God for help.

Many of the more difficult issues in this life do not have quick fixes or easy answers. Persevering through chronic physical or emotional pain requires tremendous stamina. But for me, it takes more than stamina. It takes an outside supernatural source of strength. It takes a daily connection with the fountain of life for me to be able to face life. It takes putting my faith in the one who hears my prayers and embraces me in my silence. It takes an open ear to His voice and an open heart to receive His grace for me to keep putting one foot in front of the other, minute by minute, hour by hour, day by day.

Thank you, Ginny, Tom, and Tom Junior. Your story has made Paul's words come alive for me in a new way: "God is able to make *all* grace *abound* to you, so that in *all* things at *all* times, having *all* that you need, you will *abound* in *every* good work" (2 Corinthians 9:8, emphasis mine).

Just out of curiosity, I looked up the word *abound* in the dictionary. It means "to exist in great quantities; inexhaustible." Ginny, Tom, and Tom Junior have become a spring of living water for me, filling my spirit with a renewed sense of confidence that God will be there for me through thick and thin, giving me what I need in great quantities and insulating me from despair.

Continue to let your abundant waters flow, my friends. There are more cups to fill. Indeed, you are abounding in a very great work.

In prayer, it is better to have a heart without words than words without a heart.

John Bunyan

Not in the achievement, but in the endurance of the human soul does it show its divine grandeur and its alliance with an infinite God.

Edwin Chapin

Faith will lead you where you cannot walk. Reason has never been a mountain climber.

E. W. Kenyon

Let us not underestimate how hard it is to be compassionate. Compassion is hard because it requires the inner discipline to go with others to the place where they are weak, vulnerable, lonely, and broken. But this is not our spontaneous response to suffering. What we desire most is to do away with suffering by fleeing from it or finding a quick cure for it.

Henri J. M. Nouwen

Faith is not believing that God can, but that God will!

Abraham Lincoln

Power Perks: A Sip of Hope and Humor

God will not look you over for medals, degrees, or diplomas, but for scars.

Elbert Green Hubbard

God is a Master Artist. And there are aspects of your life and character—good, quality things—he wants others to notice. So without using blatant tricks or obvious gimmicks, God brings the cool, dark contrast of suffering into your life. That contrast, laid up against the golden character of Christ within you, will draw attention…to him. Light against darkness. Beauty against affliction. Joy against sorrow. A sweet, patient spirit against pain and disappointment—major contrasts have a way of attracting attention. You are the canvas on which he paints glorious truths, sharing beauty, and inspiring others. So that people might see him.

Joni Eareckson Tada

CHAPTER 21

A Second Chance

I n the last days, God says,
I will pour out my Spirit on all people.
Your sons and daughters will prophesy,
your young men will see visions,
your old men will dream dreams.'"

Acts 2:17

I want you to meet someone. Though he is no longer living, you can come to know this man through a powerful piece of writing he left behind. I want you to hear his message because it is the ultimate pick-me-up-and-set-me-on-the-right-path story. It will energize, challenge, and change you.

First, let me give you some background. Few leaders have ever displayed the unquenchable zeal and courage that characterized William Booth. Those who knew him said that once he put his mind to task, he was like a runaway freight train—there was no stopping him. Fortunately he put his enormous drive to good use. In 1865, William and his wife, Catherine, founded the Christian Mission in London to furnish spiritual and material aid to needy people. In 1878, the mission became known as The Salvation Army. Today, there are thousands of branches of The Salvation Army established across the globe.

What was the driving force behind William Booth? What ruling principle governed his life? What kept him pressing forward against all odds? Perhaps part of the answer lies in the story that follows.

One afternoon, William Booth was graced with the ability to see into the unseen world, and what he witnessed changed every motive in his life. His story left its mark on me. Ever since I read his account a few months ago, I have not looked at my own commitments quite the same. I have a hunch you won't either.

> I had a very strange vision the other day. And I have been greatly perplexed as to whether or not I should tell it to others....
>
> In this vision I was one who was active in religious activities. In fact, I considered myself to be quite a shining light. I always attended church on Sunday and I taught in the Sunday school. Now

and then, though not very often, I visited the sick. And in addition to these good deeds I gave a little money to support Christian work.

In all this I was quite sincere. I had no idea of playing the hypocrite. It's true that I didn't stop to consider what Christianity really was, although I talked freely enough about it at times, and pitied people who didn't profess to be Christians.

I seldom, if ever, considered what Jesus Christ required. Nor was I very concerned about the lost, although I heard these matters occasionally discussed in my presence. I had gotten into a definite rut in thought and action and profession. And I went on from day to day, hoping that everything would turn out all right in the end.

But in my vision, I thought that without any apparent warning a dangerous fever seized me. I became terribly sick all of a sudden. In fact, in just a few hours I was brought to the very brink of death. This was serious business indeed. Everyone about me was in great confusion, and those who loved me were paralyzed with fear.

Some took action. The proper medicines were administered. There were consultations among several physicians. And the members of my family hurried to my side from far and near. Friends and acquaintances came.

I was given the best medical care possible—but all proved in vain.

I could feel that the medicines weren't helping.

…[But] if I did not recover, I had no reason to be terribly concerned, because, wasn't I a Christian? Hadn't I been converted? Didn't I believe the Bible? Why should I fear?…

[And then] a strange faintness seized me. I lost consciousness.

My next sensation was altogether beyond description. It was a thrill of a new and celestial existence. I was in heaven.

After the first feeling of surprise had some-what subsided, I looked around me and took in the situation. It was way beyond anything of earth—positively delightful…. No human eyes ever beheld such perfection, such beauty. No earthly ear ever heard such music…. At first I was swallowed up with a sort of ecstatic intoxication, which feeling was immediately enhanced by the consciousness that I was safe, saved, to suffer and sin no more.

And then, suddenly, a new set of feelings began to creep over me. Strange as it may seem, I felt somewhat lonely and a little sad, even in the midst of this infinite state of bliss. Because up to this moment I was alone. Not one of the bright beings who were soaring and singing in the bright ether above me, nor the ones who were hastening hither and thither, as though bent upon some high mission, had spoken to me or approached me.

I was alone in heaven! Then, in a still stranger and more mysterious way, I appeared to feel in myself a sort of unfitness for the society of those pure beings who were sailing around me in indescribable loveliness. How could it be? Had I come there by mistake? Was I not counted worthy of this glorious inheritance? It was indeed a mystery.

My thoughts went back to earth. And all before me, as though unfolded by an angel's hand, the record of my past life was unrolled before my eyes. What a record it was! I glanced over it. And in a glance I seemed to master its entire contents—so rapidly, indeed, that I became conscious of a marvelous quickening of my intellectual powers. I realized that I could take in and understand in a moment what would have required a day with my poor, darkened faculties on earth….

It described in full detail the object for which I had lived. It recorded my thoughts and feelings and actions—how and for what I had employed my time, my money, my influence, and all the other talents and gifts which God had entrusted me to spend for His glory and for the salvation of the lost….

They wrung my soul with sorrow and self-reproach, because on the "Record of Memory" I saw how I had occupied myself during the few years, which I had been allowed to live amidst all these miseries after Jesus Christ had called me to be His soldier. I was reminded how, instead of fighting His battles, instead of saving souls by bringing them to His feet, and so preparing them for admission into this lovely place, I had been, on the contrary, intent on earthly things, selfishly seeking my own, spending my life in practical unbelief, disloyalty and disobedience....

I was in anguish, strange as it may appear, considering I was in heaven. But so it was. Wondering whether there was not some comfort for me, I involuntarily looked around. And I saw a marvelous phenomenon on the horizon at a great distance. All that part of the heavens appeared to be filled with a brilliant light, surpassing the blaze of a thousand suns at noonday. And yet there was no blinding glare making it difficult to gaze upon, as is the case with our own sun when it shines in its glory. Here was a brilliance far surpassing anything that could be imagined, and yet I could look upon it with pleasure....

I realized it was coming in my direction....

Before I could prepare my spirit for the visitation, it was upon me. The King was here! In the center of circling hosts—which rose tier above tier into the blue vault above, turning on Him their millions of eyes, lustrous with the love they bore Him—I beheld the celestial form of Him who died for me upon the cross. The procession halted. Then at a word of command, they formed up instantly in three sides of a square in front of me, the King standing in the center immediately opposite the spot where I had prostrated myself.

What a sight it was! Worth toiling a lifetime to behold it!...

I was bewildered by the scene. The songs, the music, the shouts of the multitude that came like the roar of a thousand cataracts, echoed and reechoed through the sunlit mountains. And the magnificent and endless array of happy spirits ravished my senses with passionate delight. All at once, however, I remembered myself, and was reminded of the High Presence before Whom I was bowed, and lifting up my eyes I beheld Him gazing upon me....

That face, that Divine face, seemed to say to me, for language was not needed to convey to the very depths of my soul what His feelings were to me: "You will feel yourself little in harmony with these, once the companions of My tribulations and now of My glory, who counted not their lives dear to themselves, in order that they might bring honor to Me and salvation to men." And He gave a look of admiration at the host of apostles and martyrs and warriors gathered around Him.

Oh, that look of Jesus! I felt that to have one such loving recognition—it would be worth dying a hundred deaths at the stake. It would be worth being torn asunder by wild beasts. The angelic escort felt it, too, for their responsive burst of praise and song shook the very skies and the ground on which I lay....

I felt, rather than heard, Him saying to me in words that engraved themselves as fire upon my brain:

"Go back to earth. I will give you another opportunity. Prove yourself worthy of My name. Show to the world that you possess My Spirit by doing My works, and becoming, on My behalf, a savior of men. You will return here when you have finished the battle, and I will give you a place in My conquering train, and a share in My glory."

What I felt under that look and those words, no heart or mind could possibly describe. They were mingled feelings. First came the unutterable anguish arising out of the full realization that I had wasted my life, that it had been a life squandered on the paltry ambitions and trifling pleasures of earth—while it might have been filled and sown with deeds that would have produced a never-ending harvest of heavenly fruit. My life could have won for me the approval of heaven's King, and made me worthy to the companion of these glorified heroes.

But combined with this self-reproach there was a gleam of hope.... I could have the privilege of living my life over again. True, it was a high responsibility, but Jesus would be with me. His Spirit would enable me. And in my heart I felt ready to face it.

The cloud of shining ones had vanished. The music was silent. I closed my eyes and gave myself over, body, soul, and spirit, to the disposal of my Savior—to live, not for my own salvation, but for the glory of my Christ and for the salvation of the world. And then and there, the same blessed voice of my King stole over my heart, as He promised that His presence should go with me back to earth and make me more than a conqueror through His blood.[1]

When I first read William's vision, I thought of Jesus' story in Matthew 13 about the man who found the hidden treasure. Jesus was telling the disciples a parable: "The kingdom of heaven is like treasure hidden in a field. When a man found it, he hid it again, and then in his joy went and sold all he had and bought that field" (Matthew 13:44).

Can you picture it? Here is your typical, get-up-and-go-to-work kind of guy who is walking to his job as usual. And then, abruptly and completely unexpectedly, something happens—he thrusts his staff into the ground and hears *clunk*. It doesn't feel like a rock. It doesn't feel like a clump of dirt. No—it feels more like he hit one of those old-fashioned wooden barrels that hold fresh rainwater.

To get a better look, he stoops over, pokes around, and brushes some dirt to the side. Much to his astonishment, he discovers what looks like the top of a small wooden chest. Excited at his discovery, he digs with his staff, shovels with his hands, kicks with his feet, and yanks with all his might to free the box from its grave. With the sharp edge of a jagged rock, he smashes the lock securing the lid and pops the top open. Blinding sunlight flashes off the glistening pile of treasure before him: gold coins, brilliant diamonds, sparkling emeralds—all of it worth a fortune—fill the chest to its rim.

Slamming the lid shut and quickly looking in all directions, the man carefully investigates his surroundings. Is anyone nearby? Did anyone see? In haste he lowers the treasure back in the ground, carefully covers it with dirt, firmly packs down the earth, takes mental note of the location, and runs top speed to town to inquire about the field. As an honest, upright man, he can't simply walk off with the treasure. Upon learning that the land is for sale, the man goes home, sells everything he owns, and buys the field in which the treasure is buried. In one brief encounter, everything in that man's life changed. He had a completely new reference point for all of his future decisions.

The analogy is obvious. The reference point Jesus refers to here is the kingdom of heaven. It's a call to live life in light of eternity.

I believe that there are times in life when God gives us a new reference point. He brings us face-to-face with people or situations that challenge us to consider whether or not we are living our days for the sake of His kingdom. These reference points call us to look "not on what is seen, but on what is unseen. For what is seen is temporary, but what is unseen is eternal" (2 Corinthians 4:18).

The Bible talks very clearly about a day when all of us will face the Lord God. "For we will all stand before God's judgment seat. It is written: 'As surely as I live,' says the Lord, 'every knee will bow before me; every tongue will confess to God.' So then, each of us will give an account of himself to God" (Romans 14:10–12).

Because Christ already bore the punishment for our sins on the cross, the issue at the judgment of believers is not punishment. God will be looking for things to reward! These rewards will be for the work we've done on earth. Therefore, the way we live and give of ourselves is enormously important.

My friend Randy Alcorn said something that has helped me understand this truth more fully: "He who lives his life backing away from his treasures has reason to despair. He who lives his life heading toward his treasures has reason to rejoice."

Many of us spend our time and energies laying up treasures on earth. Every day that we live, we move closer to our deaths and farther away from those treasures. Jesus challenges us to reverse this process—to do an about-face and change our reference point. He wants us to turn around and face heaven—to invest our time and energies in the kingdom of heaven. That way we will constantly move toward our treasures instead of away from them.

Good news: As long as we live on earth, we have a God of second chances. We have the opportunity today to alter our priorities, change the directions of our lives, and invest our assets in the kingdom of God. The man in Jesus' parable used good judgment and took action; so did William Booth. If you were to meet Jesus tomorrow, would your "Record of Memory" show debits or credits? Why not begin today to add to your credit line?

Great will be your reward now and in heaven—because when it comes to passing out blessings, God is into double dipping!

Power Perks: A Sip of Hope and Humor

Experience is never the ground of our trust; it is the gateway to the One whom we trust.

Oswald Chambers

Vision encompasses vast vistas outside the realm of the predictable, the safe, and the unexpected.

Charles R. Swindoll

The Christians who have turned the world upside down have been men and women with a vision in their hearts and the Bible in their hands.

T. B. Maston

The LORD looks down from heaven on the entire human race; he looks to see if there is even one with real understanding, one who seeks for God.

Psalm 14:2, NLT

For this is what the high and lofty One says—he who lives forever, whose name is holy: "I live in a high and holy place, but also with him who is contrite and lowly in spirit, to revive the spirit of the lowly and to revive the heart of the contrite."

Isaiah 57:15

"'In the last days, God says, I will pour out my Spirit on all people. Your sons and daughters will prophesy, your young men will see visions, your old men will dream dreams. Even on my servants, both men and women, I will pour out my Spirit in those days…. And everyone who calls on the name of the Lord will be saved.'"

Acts 2:17–18, 21

CHAPTER 22
Touched by an Angel

Before they call I will answer.

Isaiah 65:24

After I wrote my last book, *Espresso for a Woman's Spirit: Encouraging Stories of Hope and Humor,* I had the fun of talking with TV and radio talk-show hosts across the country. One of the nice things about radio interviews is that we do them over the phone. That allows me to sit at my kitchen table in my bathrobe and sip coffee as we talk on the air during the early morning hours. Radio shows on the East Coast are three hours ahead, so when they schedule me for an 8 A.M. interview in New York, it's only 5 A.M. my time. In my opinion, that is an ungodly hour for articulate conversation, but that's the way it is, so—I thank God for espresso!

Toward the end of the media campaign, I did a talk

show in Tennessee. During the interview, the host, Beth, informed listeners that I had also written *Empty Arms*. At the close of the interview, Beth asked me to stay on the line until her break. I waited a minute or two, and then she picked up the phone. "Pam, I just have to tell you something God did for me!" she said, barely able to contain herself.

"Great!" I said, "what did He do?"

She went on to tell me about an incident that caused me to marvel once again at the goodness and grace of our loving heavenly Father. Be encouraged as you read Beth's story of God's kindness during a dark season of grief.

My husband, Bill, our four sons, and I eagerly awaited the birth of the first girl in our family, whom we had named Bethanna. It was May 8, Mother's Day, and my son Mark's birthday. But Bethanna died just minutes before she was born; a tightly twisted umbilical cord took her life before she could draw her first breath.

All of us grieved deeply. I recall lying in the recovery room, praying that God would somehow use this heart-wrenching pain for good. *What now, Lord?* I whispered through my tears.

Words from Scripture came to my mind: "The LORD has already told you what is good, and this is what he requires: to do what is right, to love mercy, and to walk humbly with your God" [Micah 6:8, NLT]. It was a verse the boys and I had memorized a while back. We had that verse inscribed on Bethanna's tombstone.

During the year that followed I felt as if God was holding me up. I drew strength from remembering His goodness to us in the past and from reading His love letters in the Bible. I also received caring attention from my friends and family, who prayed for us and helped us in whatever way they could.

But when the first anniversary of Bethanna's birth and death approached, I began to fall apart. I was agitated, distracted, and unable to concentrate on much of anything. I forgot appointments and walked around in a daze. I mentioned my plight to a friend who is a counselor, and she said, "Beth, this is normal. It's what they call anniversary grief."

She was right. After Bethanna's birthday came and went, I seemed to settle down and feel more like myself again.

Close to a year after that disturbing episode, I started asking my friends and family to pray for me. I didn't want to suffer the way I had the year before. After all, I had a husband and four sons to care for, and I needed all my faculties working well.

On the second anniversary of Bethanna's death, I was very busy with my boys. I had visited my twin sons' school for show-and-tell and delivered cookies to Mark's class so the children could help him celebrate his birthday. Next, I made a mad dash to a store to pick up some party supplies.

After gathering what I needed, I stood in line to buy some helium-filled birthday balloons for Mark. In front of me stood a beautiful young lady who was with her mother. When I first glanced at this sweet young woman, I thought, *She is so gorgeous; she looks like a movie star.* I guessed that she was in her early thirties.

As she was paying for her merchandise, she looked up at me, smiled, and then dug some money out of her purse for the cashier. I stepped up next to pay for the balloons and then noticed the young woman standing at the exit door, staring at me. I thought that was odd, but I smiled. She in turn smiled, nodded, and left the store.

As I was opening the door to my van, I noticed another van parking horizontally behind me, blocking me. I walked to the back of my van to check things out, and there was that same pretty lady walking straight toward me. She had just stepped out of her van and obviously wanted to get my attention. "I wasn't going to stop to talk to you, but my mother encouraged me to do so," she said. "I noticed the fish emblem on the back of your van. Are you a Christian?"

"Yes, I am," I replied, curious about where this conversation would lead.

"Well, you may think that I'm crazy when I tell you this," she began nervously.

"No, it's okay," I reassured her. "Go ahead."

"When I saw you in the craft store, I just knew that you

were the one I was praying for this morning. It was your face that I saw in my mind when I prayed, and I have been praying for you all day."

My jaw about hit the pavement. I was utterly flabbergasted. Here was a complete stranger telling me she had been burdened to pray for me and that the Spirit of God had shown her my face while she was praying. It wasn't your average trip-to-the-craft-store experience.

It was a short conversation. I thanked the young woman for her thoughtfulness, and she headed back to her van, where her mother was patiently waiting. "What's your name?" I called out.

"It's Lana," she yelled back, "you know, like the movie star, Lana Turner."

I chuckled and thought, *Friend, the hit television series* Touched by an Angel *needs to sign you up!* I frankly expected a dove to fly out of her van window.

When Beth finished her story, I laughed in wonder right along with her. And I was curious to know how the incident had helped her cope with her loss.

Do you know, it wasn't until late that night that Beth remembered that that day was the anniversary of Bethanna's death. But when she did, she realized that because of the events of the day, God was well aware and that He had not forgotten. He cared enough about Beth to impress a total stranger to pray for her on her most difficult day of the year. Then He orchestrated events so that their paths crossed during a mundane errand to a craft store in the middle of town. As if that weren't enough, he gave a shy young woman the courage to divulge something out of the ordinary to a complete stranger.

Wow! God is indeed a faithful and amazing God of love. And His care for you is just as deep. Watch for His surprising presence in your own daily routine. I guarantee: He's there! And He loves you!

Power Perks: A Sip of Hope and Humor

Poor little Isabel
Went to Aunty's house to play,
To wash the cups and saucers
And shoo the hens away.
She went to clean the scullery,
To dust the hearth and sweep,
But when she got to Ivyhome,
Her aunt was still asleep.
She tapped upon the windowpane
And knocked upon the door.
She knocked long her little hands
Were getting mighty sore.
"Come on in," Auntie said,
"I didn't hear you knock.
I stayed up very late last night
And forgot to set the clock."
Just then, a blast of chilly air
Came whistling through the trees.
"You'll catch your death of cold out there.
I think it's going to freeze."
Isabel watched dumfounded,
And not a word she said.
It blew the flannel nightgown
Up over Auntie's head.
Auntie didn't seem to care,
Then almost dropped her teeth
She suddenly remembered
She wore nothing underneath.

Power Perks: A Sip of Hope and Humor

She tried to act so nonchalant
And didn't give a hoot
As she stood there in the doorway
In her wrinkled birthday suit.
The old grey cat had washed her face
And stopped to lick her paw.
She hollered to the nanny goat,
"Did you see what I saw?"
The goat peered out behind a bush
To watch the episode.
It scared the critter half to death,
And she bolted down the road.
Then Isabel cleaned the scullery
With vigor and with vim
While Auntie made a pot of tea
And hummed her favorite hymn.
So if you stay at Auntie's house,
And the wind is blowing there
Be sure to take some decent clothes
And lots of underwear.[1]

John Gordon

CHAPTER 23

Lessons from the Desert

*W*ho has the wisdom to count the clouds?
  Who can tip over the water jars of the heavens
when the dust becomes hard
  and the clods of the earth stick together?

Job 38:37–38

A while back my good friend, Dr. Pamela Reeve, sent me a copy of a manuscript she was completing for publication. The title *Deserts of the Heart* immediately grabbed my attention. I thought about some of the deserts I had traveled through during my life. Oh, I'm not talking about my vacation visits to the Eastern Oregon high desert or to Arizona's picturesque Painted Desert. I'm talking about the desert experiences of my soul—those times when I've felt parched, dried up, sun scorched, and bleached of life.

If you're a card-carrying member of the human race, I know you've traveled through a desert or two yourself. You've likely had times when you've been whipped by the hot, harsh winds of life and wondered if you'd ever make it out alive. Perhaps you feel as if you're wandering aimlessly in a desert today, with so much sandy grit flying in your face that you can't even see beyond the end of your nose.

That's a fairly accurate description of where my friend Pam found herself one afternoon several years ago. And God, in a powerful and compelling way, tipped over the water jars of the heavens, flooded the parched areas of her soul with His rivers of life, and quenched her thirst. Read on, my friend, and discover His unfailing love as Pam tells her story.

A severely depressed woman had come to me for whatever counsel and help I might be able to offer. She was on her way back from an assignment in Asia and would spend a week with me before returning to her home in another part of the country. Her friends and family were deeply concerned. Alarmed. They hoped that, somehow, I might be able to help her sort through the troubling issues of her life.

I tried hard to do just that. Every moment that I wasn't working, I spent with her. I shared the Scriptures and every principle I knew. I listened to her by the hour. Our talks went far into the night. At the end of the week, however, she was no better. In fact, she seemed a great deal worse. Her depression had deepened. Her despair yawned like a bottomless crevasse in the path ahead. All of those hours with me had accomplished precisely nothing.

The morning she was to leave, I woke up with a sinking heaviness. *A lot of good you've done,* I told myself. *You haven't helped this poor woman one iota. She's leaving your home with a heavier heart than when she arrived. Let's be real, Pamela Reeve…what have you* ever *done to help anyone? You're of no use— and probably never will be. You are worthless.*

Out of habit more than desire, I picked up my daily devotional book from the nightstand. The opening Scripture for that day cut through my gray mood like the sun through parting clouds. "Again, the kingdom of heaven is like a merchant seeking beautiful pearls, who, when he had found one pearl of great price, went and sold all that he had and bought it" (Matthew 13:45–46, NKJV). Immediately, the Lord spoke to my heart. "Hear Me, My daughter. You are that pearl to Me. A pearl of great price."

I closed the book, shutting the door to my heart at the same time, unwilling to believe what He was saying. "Me? A pearl of great value?

Common river rock is more likely. I have no value at all. I'm worthless." (It wasn't the first time I had said such words.)

I took my guest to the airport for her early morning flight. The drive was mostly silent. I had nothing left to say and felt overwhelmed with a sense of failure. *She came to me for help. She needed someone. And I'm sending her away as empty as when she walked through my front door.* What had she found in my home? An oasis—or more wasteland?

When I got back home, I found a small, neatly wrapped package, which my guest had left for me on the dining-room table. *She shouldn't have done that!* I told myself. I certainly hadn't earned it! I pulled away the wrapping and opened the little box.

It was a pearl ring—the most beautiful I had ever seen. And it fit me to perfection.

As I slipped the ring onto my finger, the Lord spoke to my heart again. *Say what you will. Imagine what you like. Shut Me out if you can. My gift cannot be earned, only given. Yet I tell you once again, you are a pearl of great price in My eyes. You are My beloved.*

His beloved! This time, I drank it in. This time, I let His words seep into the parched soil of my soul. What refreshing waters began to pour forth from that deep pool in my oasis. I wore the pearl ring day and night for many years. It remains my most precious possession. Each time I look at it, I am reminded, "You are God's beloved, a pearl of great price. He gave His life to purchase you."

When feelings of worthlessness steal across my soul like afternoon shadows, I look at the pearl and remind myself, *You are beloved. Yes—you!*

There is nothing more wonderful in time or eternity than to know that you are deeply and perfectly loved. It is sweet, cold water for the deepest thirst of your heart. It is the spring that bubbles up to bring life to your desert. The great inexhaustible aquifer beneath you is the Lord's intense love for you, just as you are. He is a never-changing, never-failing source of love.[1]

The Weary Traveler

The Weary Traveler collapsed in the middle of the rocky road. Hanging his head in defeat, he buried his face in his hands and cried, "Lord, I just can't go any further. I'm too tired. I give up!"

Jesus knelt beside the Weary Traveler, placing a gentle hand on his shoulder. "Look!" Jesus encouraged, pointing to the path just ahead. "It isn't as steep. There are fewer rocks and smaller potholes. If you look farther into the distance, you can see that the path is smooth, surrounded by towering shade trees, rippling brooks, and flowers bursting with color. There's a nice place to stop and rest just around the bend. I know—I've taken this path before."

Shaking his head in dismay, the Weary Traveler sighed, "I can't go one step further. My strength is gone. I just can't make it. It's no use."

"But look!" Jesus said, pointing to the path behind them. The ground they had covered was dangerously steep, strewn with heavy, sharp boulders, deeper than a man is tall. "We've come so far. Don't give up now. To do so would be like building a house and then burning it to the ground."

The Weary Traveler began to weep. "I'm just too exhausted. I can't."

Power Perks: A SIP OF HOPE AND HUMOR

Jesus smiled at the Weary Traveler, placed His hands tenderly around his face, lifting his eyes to His. Jesus' eyes radiated a warmth and love that washed over the Weary Traveler like a sunbeam. With deep, unlimited compassion, Jesus reassured him: "You don't have to do it alone. Lean on me. I'll help you."

The Weary Traveler's tears slowed. He looked hopefully into Jesus' eyes, and with the last vestige of strength left in his body, reached out his arms to Jesus. Jesus took hold of his hands, pulled him to his feet, and firmly planted His arm around the Traveler's waist. Every time he stumbled, Jesus held him up. Whenever he started to veer off course, Jesus guided him back to the center of the path. When the sun beat down upon them and the Weary Traveler's mouth was parched dry, Jesus gave him refreshing, cool water.

"Thank You, Lord. I couldn't do any of this without You," the Weary Traveler said, wiping his mouth with a slight smile.

Jesus laughed with delight. "This is what I love doing most, My child. I was sent to help you find your way home. We'll take it slow. There will likely be unexpected detours along the way, but as long as you stick with Me, we'll get there. And that, my good friend, is a promise that cannot be broken."[2]

Mandy Gordon

Koffee Klatch Questions

I have designed the following questions for people who want to talk through the joys and challenges of life with their friends, perhaps over a freshly brewed cup of coffee. Groups of two to six trusted friends can have stimulating discussions and experience personal growth. Knowing that we are not alone and hearing how others manage life's tests can be very empowering.

I encourage you to use these Koffee Klatch Questions as a springboard for sharing and building relationships with others. Strive for authenticity as you connect with others, and watch the marvelous ways God shows up and meets your needs. Jesus said, "Where two or more are gathered in my name, I am there in the midst of them."

CHAPTER 1: STARSTRUCK

1. How did your family of origin typically explain an unusual turn of events? Was it a coincidence, happenstance, divine encounter? Or did they view it in some other way?

2. Tell your group about a time in your life when you were amazed by a turn of events that seemed out of the ordinary. Perhaps you may recall a specific answer to prayer or a fulfilled longing.

CHAPTER 2: JUST TO KEEP THINGS PERCOLATIN'
1. Give your friends a laugh by sharing a funny incident that happened to you or someone you know.

2. What will you do this week to add a bit more fun and games into your daily life? Make sure that your goal is concrete and measurable.

CHAPTER 3: A RISK WORTH TAKING
1. A key point in this chapter is that good relationships don't grow in the absence of conflict; they grow in the presence of a reconciling spirit. How have you seen this principle at work in your life?

2. When you read this story, did you sense the Holy Spirit bringing to mind someone in your sphere of influence? Is He nudging you to reach out? Talk about it with the group.

CHAPTER 4: FROM FOREIGNER TO FRIEND
1. Tell the group about one of your prized friendships— how you met, what that person means to you, and how he or she has blessed your life.

2. God extends compassion to us and longs for us to be compassionate with others. Is there someone with whom you can share a cup of compassion this week? How and when will you follow through?

CHAPTER 5: TP FROM HEAVEN
1. Talk about a time when you asked God to meet a very specific need and what followed.

2. What specific need do you have today? Share that need with your group, and then allow them the privilege of praying for you.

CHAPTER 6: WHEN YOUR GET-UP-AND-GO GETS UP AND DIES
1. What replenishes your energy reserves when your get-up-and-go gets up and dies?

2. Is there someone who has invested time and energy in your life to whom you could offer a word of encouragement? A letter like Bert's might make his or her day. To whom will you write, and when will you mail it?

CHAPTER 7: IS IT TIME TO CATCH THE WAVE?
1. Can you recall a time in your life when you sensed stirrings in your soul that said something was about to change? Tell the story to your group.

2. Have you ever prayed like Dr. Steve did, *Lord, if there is something more you have for me to do, please show me, and I'll do it?* If so, what has transpired since then? If not, would you consider saying that prayer today? Why or why not?

CHAPTER 8: BIG PLANS FOR A LITTLE BOY
1. Do you recall a season in your life when it was difficult to "keep the faith"? Describe it to the group.

2. What helped you endure that difficult season, and what did you learn in the midst of that dark time?

CHAPTER 9: APRIL FOOLS
1. How about adding some laughter to a loved one's day by planning a harmless prank? Perhaps you can brainstorm some ideas in your group.

2. Think of one concrete way you can squeeze a few more drops of joy out of today. What's your plan?

CHAPTER 10: AN ANGEL BEHIND EVERY DESK
1. Andrew's story underlines the reality of God's attentiveness to our needs. What concern weighing heavy on your heart today needs God's attention? Tell the group and allow others to pray for you.

2. Andrew's goal was to become a mighty man of God. What step can you take to grow stronger in your faith?

CHAPTER 11: GENTLE INVITATIONS

1. What kind of situation typically leads you to pray? What hinders you from praying?

2. Share a prayer request with your group, and take some time to pray for one another before you leave.

CHAPTER 12: THE MILE-WIDE SPACE IN THE MIDDLE OF THE BED

1. Do you ever struggle with the Pharisee Syndrome? When does it typically creep in and get the best of you?

2. Tell about a time in your life when you forgave another and the results of doing so.

CHAPTER 13: HOLIDAZE

1. Ever had a hair-raising holiday? Tell the group what happened.

2. How do you reduce stress and make more room for peace and fun during the holiday season? Share some tips that have worked, and make a collective list among the people in your small group. Use the tip sheet as you approach the next holiday season.

CHAPTER 14: HANDYMAN HORRORS

1. In what areas of your life is it easy to be self-sufficient?

2. What challenge are you facing that has drained your resources? Please describe it to the group and then pray together, asking God to step in and help you.

CHAPTER 15: A MIRACLE IN THE THIRD ROW

1. There were times when Charonne felt inadequate in her ability to love Jennifer. Is there someone in your life about whom you feel the same? Using discretion, talk about the nature of your challenge.

2. One of the secrets to Charonne's healing influence in Jennifer's life was the daily prayer she offered for the little girl. Whom would you like to pray for on a daily basis this week? Why not post that person's initials on a card in your wallet or on the bathroom mirror as a reminder to pray?

CHAPTER 16: A DREAM COME TRUE

1. Your dreams matter to God. Tell the group about one dream you have for your own life. Then allow them to pray for you toward the fulfillment of that dream.

2. What dreams have you already seen come to pass in your life? Share them with the group.

CHAPTER 17: CAN I FILL THAT CUP FOR YOU?

1. Like me, do you ever have moments of fatigue when you wonder if you're doing anybody any good? How do you usually deal with those troubling thoughts?

2. What situations have shot holes in the bottom of your cup recently?

CHAPTER 18: GARAGE SALE TREASURES
1. Ask the Lord to bring to mind one person who needs a touch of His love and care through you. Who comes to mind?

2. How do you plan to follow through?

CHAPTER 19: ADOLESCENT ESCAPADES
1. What is one target you are shooting for at this time of your life?

2. Proverbs 12:14 says, "The deeds of a man's hands will return to him." How has this been true in your life?

CHAPTER 20: GOD HEARS YOUR SILENCE, AND HE SPEAKS
1. With what part of this story did you most identify?

2. Can you tell your group about a time in your life when you sensed that the Lord was giving you specific direction?

CHAPTER 21: A SECOND CHANCE
1. What were your thoughts about your own life after reading William Booth's story?

2. What could you do this week to invest in God's kingdom?

CHAPTER 22: TOUCHED BY AN ANGEL

1. Have you or has someone close to you ever experienced "anniversary grief"? What helped you or your loved one cope?

2. It took courage for Lana to tell Beth what she was thinking. Why not ask the Lord to give you the strength to offer encouraging words to someone this week? Then be very sensitive to the people He brings across your path, and by all means, speak up.

CHAPTER 23: LESSONS FROM THE DESERT

1. Talk about a desert experience in your life. What were the circumstances that led you into the desert?

2. What did you learn during that time that might be helpful to a weary traveler who is currently in the desert?

Multnomah Publishers®

The publisher and author would love to hear your comments about this book. *Please contact us at:*
www.multnomah.net/espresso

Notes

CHAPTER 4

1. William Johnson, "And Smile, Smile, Smile," *Sports Illustrated,* 4 June 1973, 78.

CHAPTER 6

1. Adapted from Clark Cothern, *Detours* (Sisters, Ore.: Multnomah Books, 1999), 127–36.

CHAPTER 8

1. M. Scott Peck, *The Road Less Traveled* (New York: Simon and Schuster, 1978), 16.

CHAPTER 10

1. Max Lucado, "Classic and Contemporary Excerpts," *Christianity Today,* 8 December 1997, 53.

CHAPTER 12

1. Henri Nouwen, *The Road to Daybreak: A Spiritual Journey* (New York: Doubleday, 1988), 64–6.

CHAPTER 18

1. Steve Farrar, *Point Man* (Sisters, Ore.: Multnomah Publishers, 1994).

CHAPTER 21

1. This story was adapted from a tract published in the early 1900s by Life Messengers, Seattle, Washington. Public domain.

CHAPTER 22

1. Poem by John Gordon © 1995. Used by permission.

CHAPTER 23

1. Pamela Reeve, *Deserts of the Heart* (Sisters, Ore.: Multnomah Books, 2001), 110–3.

2. Mandy Gordon, "The Weary Traveler" © 2000. Used by permission.

Enjoy spiritual energy throughout the day with stories from *Pam Vredevelt*

Espresso for Your Spirit

In engaging, humorous, and often poignant vignettes, bestselling author Pam Vredevelt serves up cup after cup of energizing espresso to encourage the spirits of overwhelmed and exhausted parents.

ISBN 1-57673-485-4

Espresso for a Woman's Spirit

Exhaustion doesn't have to be habit-forming—overcome it with humorous and poignant vignettes that bring refreshment to the soul the way espresso brings energy to the body.

ISBN 1-57673-636-9

In your darkest place, you may find a glimpse of glory

Angel

Behind

the
Rocking

Stories of Hope in Unexpected Places

Chair

Pam Vredevelt

Brimming with moving personal stories, *Angel Behind the Rocking Chair* offers hope and encouragement to those facing unexpected adversity. Each story is a reassuring reminder of God's unfailing love.

ISBN 1-57673-644-X

Hope and Support for Those Who Have Suffered a Miscarriage, Stillbirth, or Tubal Pregnancy
by Pam Vredevelt

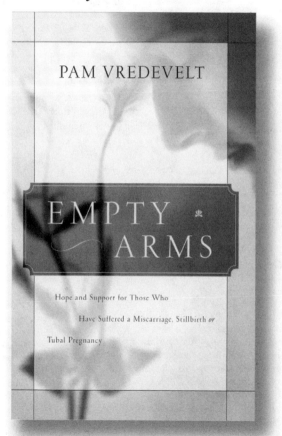

Having lost a child, the author writes with compassionate insight to women (and their families), addressing grief, anger, guilt, spiritual battles, and other pertinent topics.

ISBN 1-57673-851-5